Must say I enjoyed the manuscript thoroughly and am sur~~~~~~~~~~~~~~~~~~~ resource for boards. It's certainly much better than a great deal of what is out there now. I love the way it is organized, the readable style and depth of content. The very effective use of case illustrations and quick tips adds a great deal. It is also way above average in recognizing that 'one size does not necessarily fit all'.
Vic Murray, Adjunct Professor, School of Public Administration, University of Victoria;
former Director, School of Nonprofit Management, York University;
recipient of 2002 ARNOVA Life Time Achievement Award.

I have worked on boards at both the national and local levels for some time and wish that a book of this clarity and depth had been available for both my personal use as a board member and for my use as a consultant to agencies in the sector. It deals with complicated processes in a clear manner and gives useful examples and tips for boards and their members.
Allan Rix, Founding/Managing Director, Center for Voluntary Sector
Research and Development, Carleton University, Ottawa (CVSRD);
and recent Board Chair, Volunteer Canada.

This is an excellent book. Our board found the presentation of board types very illuminating. I'd get copies for members of my board and I'd recommend it to others as a highly valuable resource.
Raymond Lemay, Executive Director, Services for Families and Children, Prescott-Russell, Ontario;
author of numerous journal articles and book reviews;
co-author with Robert Flynn of "A Quarter Century of Normalization and Social Role Valorization: Evolution and Impact."

Governing for Results is an excellent guide to new board members interested in being truly effective in their governance role. At the same time, it is a wonderful desk reference to more experienced board members. The book blends key knowledge with skills, practical tips and case studies readers can use to reflect upon their own practices.
Mark Lalonde, Program Director, Law Enforcement and Regulatory Training Programs,
Police Academy, Justice Institute of BC.

This is, without qualification, the best handbook or guide to good governance I have read. Any type of board should be concerned with 'results'. But what I have found most challenging in my consulting to boards is to get them to understand what it means to be results-driven. Whatever type of board they are, results and knowing how assess them, are critical. The treatment of board responsibilities in this book is the best I have ever seen on the subject.
James B. Sellers, Consultant in Governance and Organizational Development, Calgary

Great book! I found it to be exceptionally thorough, practical and user-friendly. It would be a great primer, guide and 'go-to' manual for directors, particularly those of nonprofit organizations but also for-profit as well.
Ron Robertson, Managing Partner, Ray Berndtson Robertson Surette, Ottawa, Executive Search;
Board member, Community Foundation of Ottawa.

< ZEN >

GOVERNING FOR RESULTS

If you don't know where you are, and
You don't know where you're going,
Any road will get you there!
But how will you know 'if'
Or 'when' you've arrived
Or made any progress at all?

GOVERNING FOR RESULTS

A Director's Guide to Good Governance

Mel D. Gill

Book design, typesetting: Roy Diment VRG
www.members.shaw.ca/vrg
Cover, Roy Diment

Note for Librarians: a cataloguing record for this book that includes Dewey Decimal Classification and US Library of Congress numbers is available from the National Library of Canada. The complete cataloguing record can be obtained from the National Library's online database at:
www.nlc-bnc.ca/amicus/index-e.html

ISBN 978-1-4120-4938-2

Printed in Victoria, BC, Canada

TRAFFORD

Offices in Canada, USA, Ireland, UK and Spain
This book was published *on-demand* in cooperation with Trafford Publishing. On-demand publishing is a unique process and service of making a book available for retail sale to the public taking advantage of on-demand manufacturing and Internet marketing. On-demand publishing includes promotions, retail sales, manufacturing, order fulfilment, accounting and collecting royalties on behalf of the author.
Book sales in Europe:
Trafford Publishing (UK) Ltd., Enterprise House, Wistaston Road Business Centre, Wistaston Road, Crewe CW2 7RP UNITED KINGDOM
phone 01270 251 396 (local rate 0845 230 9601)
facsimile 01270 254 983; info.uk@trafford.com
Book sales for North America and international:
Trafford Publishing, 6E–2333 Government St.,
Victoria, BC V8T 4P4 CANADA
phone 250 383 6864 (toll-free 1 888 232 4444)
fax 250 383 6804; email to bookstore@trafford.com

www.trafford.com/robots/04-2746.html

10 9 8 7 6 5 4 3

CONTENTS

ACKNOWLEDGEMENTS

This book is dedicated to the memory of my father, Henry Gill, who was always my best friend, and my mother, Edna Gill, who repeatedly prodded me with the question: "Is your book finished yet?" Well, here it is Mom!

My friends and former colleagues Helen Pigeon and Raymond Lemay, regularly encouraged me to complete the manuscript and offered excellent early advice on the structure and contents of the manuscript. My brother, Royce Gill, made valuable observations on an early draft and reminded me that the most important job of a board is to recruit, support and evaluate a competent CEO. My wife, Judith, repeatedly encouraged me to finish this book so that we could get on with other aspects of our lives.

Other colleagues made much appreciated suggestions for improvement of the manuscript and offered cover commentary. Those comments are noted on the first inside page and the back cover of this book. The many others whose work is cited in this book established the solid research and theoretical foundation upon which this director's guide is based. Thanks also to those who participated in the case studies and other research cited in the book.

Thanks also to Norah McClintock for her valuable assistance in editing the final manuscript.

PREFACE

"What's the role of the board?"
"What is expected of me as a director?"
"What personal liabilities might I risk by serving on this board?"
"What difference do governing boards really make to organizations?"
"What is governance anyway?"
"How can a board 'add value' to an organization's efforts to achieve its goals?"
"How can we evaluate the performance of the board?"
"What's the right 'governance model' for my organization?
  In fact, what is a governance model and what models are there?"
"What about Carver's policy governance model?"

These are some of the questions I have repeatedly heard from board members, senior managers, funders and other stakeholders during the past ten to fifteen years.

Numerous scandals in high-profile nonprofit and business corporations in North America over the past several decades have been attributed to failed board oversight and have spurred demands for more effective and accountable governance. Aggressive promotion of the policy governance model prompted many boards and executives to attempt to implement it. Many who tried it found that it was simply not a comfortable fit for their organization. As a result, they 'mixed and matched' it with other models and practices without any systematic rationale.

My own research, management and consulting experience has led me to conclude that the essentials of good governance are generally not well understood and that what is understood is not well communicated to the millions of volunteers who serve as directors of boards. My research also revealed that many board members share common concerns about their roles and allowed me to identify some clear indicators of boards in trouble.

A note on terminology:

♦ Executive director and chief executive officer (CEO) are used interchangeably in this book to refer to the most senior management person in the organization, regardless of title.

♦ Although the correct legal term for a member of the board of a corporation is 'director', the terms director and board member are used interchangeably in this book. Some organizations may use other terms such as trustees, commissioners or governors.

COMMON CONCERNS OF BOARD MEMBERS

According to a recent study on the governance of 20 Canadian nonprofit organizations,[1] board members commonly express concerns in four areas: the functioning of the board itself; the relationship between the board and staff; planning; and finances. The concerns identified most often are listed below.

Concerns about the board itself include how to:

- limit personal liability of directors;
- shift governance practices from an 'operational' to a 'policy' focus;
- add value (i.e., how to fully exploit the talents of board members);
- evaluate the effectiveness of governance and services;
- deal with board members who are not 'pulling their weight';
- improve succession planning for both board and staff;
- deal with community criticism; this is a particular concern for directors of organizations with statutory mandates in the areas of health, education, police services, child protection, etc.;
- increase the board's involvement in advocacy; and
- deal with volunteer fatigue and staff burnout.

Concerns about the relationship between board and staff include how to:

- develop clarity between the respective roles of board and staff;
- increase the board's focus on *'results'* rather than on operational detail; and
- reduce excessive demands on the executive director.

Concerns about planning include how to:

- improve long-term planning;
- ensure that mandates remain responsive to changes in community demographics and infrastructure;
- respond to increased pressure for community service integration and the development of integrated service delivery models;
- build stronger relationships and communicate more effectively with key internal and external stakeholders;
- and whether to, collaborate with organizations that may be in competition for the same scarce project funds; and
- achieve a balance between broad-based input and efficient decision-making.

Concerns about finances include how to:

- remain financially viable (i.e., how to strengthen, stabilize, and broaden the funding base);
- respond to increasing demands for service with shrinking financial resources;
- survive the withdrawal or absence of core or sustaining funding;
- ensure that board members have a working understanding of financial statements;
- adopt and adapt business-like and entrepreneurial practices to ensure efficiency and diversify revenues and how to do so without alienating staff (who may have a human services values set) or jeopardizing nonprofit status; and
- provide services economically in an increasingly unionized environment.

SIGNS OF A BOARD IN TROUBLE

One or more of the following warning signs almost always characterize boards and organizations that are heading for serious trouble. These warning signs were evident at some point during the recent history of one or more of the 20 Canadian nonprofit organizations in that same study.[2] These warning signs are listed below.

Human resources warning signs include:

- rapid turnover of CEOs (this was an unmistakable sign in several cases);
- frequent and substantial turnover of board members; and
- difficulty recruiting or retaining credible board members.

Financial and organizational performance warning signs include:

- chronic unplanned and/or unmanaged deficits;
- rapid depletion of reserve funds;
- a call for an outside audit or operational review by funders or other key stakeholders; and
- persistent failure to meet individual or organizational performance targets.

Meetings warning signs include:

- poor attendance at board and committee meetings;
- low level of participation in discussions at meetings; and
- poorly managed meetings, e.g., lack of focus, agendas circulated late, members unprepared.

Warning signs related to board culture include:

- underground communications, e.g., lots of 'corridor talk' and political maneuvering outside the meetings;
- unaddressed distrust among board members or between the board and CEO;
- poor communication between the CEO and the board chair or the full board;
- unresolved conflicts within the board;
- conflict of interest issues that are not confronted;
- board members feeling removed from 'what's going on in the organization';
- board divided into 'insiders' (core decision-makers) and 'outsiders';
- board dividing into factions; and
- growing minority of disaffected board members.

Decision-making warning signs include:

- regular 'rubber-stamping' of CEO recommendations without meaningful debate;
- preoccupation with operational detail rather than 'big picture' issues;
- board interference in operational detail, particularly personnel and collective bargaining;
- poor communication with key stakeholders;
- board members ignoring or circumventing board policies and decisions;
- CEO ignoring or circumventing board policies and decisions; and
- decision deadlock or paralysis.

If you share any of these common concerns of board members, or if your board or organization is showing any of the common warning signs of a board headed for trouble, this book can help you. It is organized in a way that makes it easy to find advice and information on your most pressing issues without losing a sense of the overall context of board governance. Skip directly to Part 7 for an overview of the essential elements of governing for results. Skim the 'Quick Tips' boxes (like the one below) and Case Illustrations[3] for the do's and don'ts of effective governance. Start with these Quick Tips:

Quick Tips

- ♦ Screen prospective board members carefully to ensure that you get the best skills and motivation fit possible.
- ♦ Ensure that directors understand that their first responsibility is to your organization rather than to their 'constituents'.
- ♦ Get your board focused on results, i.e., on effectiveness and efficiency measures.

- ♦ Organize committees around board rather than management responsibilities (except in the case of management or operational boards, as noted in Part 2.2 and Appendix A).
- ♦ Define as clearly as possible the respective roles of board and CEO within a full partnership.
- ♦ Manage the interface between roles flexibly, constructively, and with candor and good humor.
- ♦ Ensure that the board maintains sufficient independence from management to exercise its audit functions objectively.

Although this book is intended to fill a gap in the resources available to volunteer members of nonprofit boards of directors, much of its guidance will also be useful for directors of public and private sector corporations. The strong research base underpinning this work also makes it of interest to researchers, academics and consultants. It adds perspective to the debate about governance models and offers guidance to board members with respect to board structure, responsibilities, governance practices and problems that commonly afflict boards. It is designed as a user-friendly guide for busy directors and executives who want concise, compact and well-researched answers to perennially troubling questions about governance, the role of boards and their relationship to staff.

This book is also designed to help boards interpret the results of their responses to the Governance Self-Assessment Checklist, (GSAC) developed by the author. Its basic structure is similar to that of the Checklist and will support boards committed to strengthening their governance practices. For more information on the Governance Self-Assessment Checklist, please visit www.synergyassociates.ca.

A CD ROM, available with volume purchases of this book, contains a sample bylaw, a comprehensive set of governance policies and more detailed terms of reference for committees that may be readily adapted to any organization's needs. The sample governance policy includes detailed descriptions of the roles of board officers and the executive director. The CD ROM also contains board and director self-assessment instruments. See Appendix D for details.

Part One – Governance Basics

1.1 Governance in context

1.1.1 What is governance?

Governance may be defined as *the exercise of authority, direction and control of an organization in order to ensure that its purpose is achieved*. It refers to who is in charge of what; who sets the direction and the parameters within which the direction is to be pursued; who makes decisions about what; who sets performance indicators, monitors progress and evaluates results; and who is accountable to whom for what. Governance includes the structures, responsibilities and processes that the board of an organization uses to direct and manage its general operations. These structures, processes and organizational traditions determine how authority is exercised, how decisions are made, how stakeholders have their say and how decision-makers are held to account.

Governance may be alternatively expressed as: "A process of providing strategic leadership (by) setting direction, making policy and strategy decisions, overseeing and monitoring organizational performance, and ensuring overall accountability." [4]

The four key components of governance[5] are:

- *Accountability*: the capacity of electors (owners) and other key stakeholders to call decision-makers to account for their actions. Effective accountability has two components: 'answerability' and 'consequences'. The first is the requirement to respond periodically to questions concerning one's official actions. The second is the need for the application of sanctions for breach of rules.
- *Transparency*: timely access by electors and other key stakeholders to low-cost, relevant, reliable information about finances, products or services and management of resources.
- *Predictability*: refers to the conduct or actions of elected officials (board members) and appointed staff. Predictability results primarily from laws, regulations and role definitions that are clear, known in advance, fair, and uniformly and effectively enforced.
- *Participation* (or engagement): the involvement of electors and other key stakeholders in planning, decision processes and evaluation. This allows the board to obtain reliable information, serves as a reality check and watchdog, spurs operational efficiency, and provides feedback by users of public services necessary for monitoring access to and quality of services.

These four components are essential for the development of a culture of openness, trust and stakeholder confidence that will inspire commitment to an organization's purpose, encourage excellence in governance and nurture a healthy balance between stability and innovation.

1.1.2   Why does governance matter?

The nonprofit sector in both Canada and the United States is large and diverse. According to a recent survey[6] there were 161,227 nonprofit and voluntary organizations in Canada in 2003, 56 percent of which were registered charities. This figure does not include unincorporated associations other than registered charities. Approximately 84 percent of registered charities were incorporated. Seventy-three percent of nonprofit and voluntary organizations provide service directly to benefit the Canadian public, including health; education and research; religion; social and legal services; community development and environment; arts, culture and recreation; and philanthropy. They had annual revenues of $112 billion, constituting 8.9% of Canada's Gross Domestic Product. One-third of this revenue ($37 million) was reported by hospitals, universities and colleges, which employ 34 percent of paid staff but comprise only 1 percent of the total number of organizations. Approximately 62 percent reported annual revenues of less than $100,000 and about 80 percent reported revenues of less than $250,000. Forty-nine per cent of their revenues derive from various levels of government (mainly provincial).

Nonprofits employed over 2 million Canadians and garnered 2 billion hours of volunteer time (equivalent to one million full-time staff) from some 19 million volunteers. Nine percent of these volunteer hours were devoted to governance of the organizations. The average age of these organizations was 29 years. "Economically, the voluntary sector in Canada in 1997 was comparable in size to the economy of the province of British Columbia"[7]

The 'independent sector' in the United States was comprised of 1.2 million organizations (including religious organizations) in 1998. Together, these organizations had revenues of $664.8 billion in 1997 and employed 7.1 percent of working Americans. Forty-two percent of the independent sector jobs were in health, 21.6 percent in education and research, 11.6 percent in religious organizations and 17.5 percent in social and legal services. The efforts of American voluntary sector organizations were supported by 109.4 million volunteers and were estimated to be worth $225.9 billion. The combined value of these organizations was approximately 6.7 percent of the Gross National Income.[8]

These organizations depend on volunteer boards of directors to set direction, guide them towards fulfillment of their missions and objectives, and account to a broad spectrum of stakeholders, including members, donors, funders, clients, and the general public. Effective governance of these organizations is therefore clearly in the public interest.

Over the past two decades, however, public attention has been repeatedly drawn to failures in corporate governance. The United Way of America, the Canadian Red Cross, the National Arts Centre, the International Olympic Committee, and the B.C. Ferries Corporation, among others, have all experienced high-profile crises in recent years. These failures have eroded public confidence in nonprofit institutions in general and led to a call for greater transparency and public accountability.

The *Cadbury Report,* commissioned by the London Stock Exchange in the United Kingdom in 1992, and the *Dey Report,* commissioned by the Toronto Stock Exchange in 1994, both highlighted the problems in corporate governance in the 'for-profit' sector. The BreX bankruptcy in the early nineties in Canada and the recent Enron and WorldCom collapses in the U.S are examples of poor governance and poor management in the private sector. In 2002, the United States Congress passed the Sarbanes-Oxley Act in an attempt to impose a 'rules-based' (rather than 'principles-based') regulatory framework on corporate boards to lessen the future risk of such disasters. In Canada, the 1999 *'Broadbent Report',* commissioned by the Voluntary Sector Roundtable, highlighted governance and accountability concerns in the Canadian voluntary sector. The Auditor General of Canada and provincial counterparts have commented extensively during the past decade on the importance of good governance practices to ensure effective organizational performance and accountability for efficient expenditure of public funds.[9]

Governing boards carry the trust of the public, as well as of the members, owners and share/ stakeholders of the organization. They provide an accountability structure for management. The importance of good governance grows with the level of public interest and investment in an organization. Although there is ample anecdotal evidence that the work of nonprofits usually continues in spite of flawed governance; the job still gets done! Yet there is also evidence that governing boards can enhance organizational performance by understanding and undertaking the governance role in a manner suitable for their particular organization.

Research increasingly supports the long-held conventional wisdom that good governance practices are important to effective organizational performance. But, for the most part, the research suggests that the relationship between good governance and organizational effectiveness is correlative rather than causal[10]; in other words, where we find the former, we also tend to find the latter. It cannot be definitively said that good governance *leads to* organizational effectiveness. However, a study conducted by the Conference Board of Canada[11] three years after the publication of the Toronto Stock Exchange report, "Where Were the Directors? Guidelines for Improved Corporate Governance in Canada," found that corporations that had implemented the recommended best governance practices had attained the best results on key performance criteria. Similarly, among Canadian corporations with more than $300 million in capitalization, the 25 that were identified as the "best governed" had achieved a 74% three-year return on investment, compared with a 19% return for the 25 worst governed corporations.[12]

These studies suggest that high performance boards are more likely to have:

- A high degree of involvement in strategic planning and setting the organization's mission;
- A focus on the needs of clients or consumers;
- A positive relationship with key stakeholders;
- A high degree of key stakeholder agreement on mission and values;
- A focus on results;

- A process for monitoring achievement of objectives;
- Competent board and staff leadership;
- Sufficient independence from management to make objective decisions based on sound information that is systematically gathered;
- Effective use of resources;
- Financial stability;
- Clear lines of accountability;
- An organizational culture that encourages good teamwork, respect for organizational norms, values staff and encourages excellence;
- A commitment to board self-evaluation and development;
- A good balance between stability and flexible, innovative and adaptive responses to environmental changes; and,
- Perceived legitimacy and credibility.

1.1.3   Three basic organizational functions – work, management and governance

Before one can understand where governance fits within an organization, one must first understand the basic functions essential to operating and maintaining an organization. Cyril Houle, an early authority on boards, identified the three basic tasks of an organization as "the work to be done, the administration of that work, and the establishment of policies to guide it. The work is done by the staff, the administration by management, and policy-making (or governance) by the board."[13]

- The *Work* is what needs to be done to achieve the basic mission of the organization. It is why the organization exists. Without this, there is no need for management or governance.
- *Management* of the work becomes increasingly important as an organization increases in size and complexity.
- *Governance* is the establishment and safeguarding of the organization's mission and the general oversight of its direction.

Figure 1 provides this author's approximation of the relative importance of these three functions in fulfilling the purpose of an organization. The percentages are rough approximations of the proportionate range of an organization's resources devoted to the respective functions. The actual percentages may vary according to the type and size of organization and to the different stages in the organization's development.

Figure 1: Relative Allocation of resources to key organizational functions

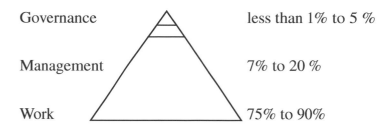

Governance   less than 1% to 5 %

Management   7% to 20 %

Work   75% to 90%

While Houle calls for each role to be delineated as clearly as possible, he acknowledges that the interrelationship between them may require a 'zone of accommodation' between the parties. Responsibility for some issues may overlap. In these cases, constructive accommodation will be needed. However, the board has legal primacy. It is the board that "has put the executive (senior manager) where he/she is, has set the conditions of his/her work, and, if it wishes can replace him/her"…although the board is in a somewhat "shadowy dim light at the back of *the organizational stage*."[14]

One of the objectives of this handbook is to shed more light on the 'organizational stage' upon which the work, management and governance of organizations are played out in the day-to-day drama of human interaction in real organizations.

The governance function is fundamental to establishing the purpose of an organization, providing direction and accountability, and ensuring its success or failure. Its overall importance to stakeholders increases in relation to the degree of public or stakeholder investment or interest in the organization and to the size and complexity of the organization. That is, governance increases in importance with the number of people engaged in, or potentially affected by, the activities of an organization and the degree of public, donor, beneficiary or consumer investment in it.

A significant majority of nonprofit corporations in North America has very few or no staff. In these organizations, board members often become involved in some management or work functions in addition to governance. Within a short span of time, board members may wear all three hats – they may make a decision to develop a major donor program (governance), reconcile the month's accounts (management), and design an event leaflet (work). This is particularly true of organizations in the early stages

Case Illustration – A board that wears three hats

A Lions Club in rural Saskatchewan has raised an average of $15,000 annually for the past 40 years. Its executive committee (board) is responsible for the governance of the organization and, in consultation with club members, sets the programs and events that form the focus of its fundraising efforts. The treasurer 'manages' the finances; he keeps the books and writes the checks. Board members collaborate on the 'staff' work of designing and promoting fundraising events.

of development and those that, because of the nature of their work or resources, remain relatively small.[15]

Involvement of board members in management or in day-to-day operational work becomes less appropriate, less practical and less functional as organizations acquire staff and financial resources to undertake and manage the organization's work.

Case Illustration: Too much board involvement in management

Several board members of an Association for Community Living (with an annual budget of $10 million) were parents of the organization's developmentally handicapped clients. These board members micro-managed programs and reported directly to the board. This undermined the executive director's efforts to manage certain programs and staff. Ironically, the board had had some training in the policy governance model and, although there was no board minute on the decision, some board members and executive directors were operating under the belief that the board had adopted this model. The confusion over roles and the failure of the board to implement governance practices better suited to the size of the organization resulted in turnover of seven executive directors in 10 years. The resulting organizational instability gave unionized staff the upper hand in playing off board members against management.

1.1.4   Why do we need boards?

Any organization seeking incorporation under federal and/or provincial or state legislation is required to have a board of directors and a set of bylaws. Incorporated and unincorporated organizations that have a constitution may be eligible for registration as charities for tax exemption purposes. The board of directors is selected by the organization's membership or controlling stakeholders and is mandated to oversee the organization, management and performance of the work of the organization. The board of directors is a legally constituted corporate entity that:

- Has a separate legal personality under the law;
- Can be held accountable under the law for the performance and actions of the organization;
- Carries the share/stakeholders' (owners, members, electors, investors) and public trust and accountability on behalf of the organization it governs;
- Represents the interests of share/stakeholders and the public to the organization, and vice versa;
- Sets or approves the general direction and financing of the organization;
- Can protect the directors from personal liability for certain actions of the corporation;
- Develops or maintains the organization's mission;

- Selects, supports, evaluates and, if necessary, terminates the senior manager;
- Provides advice to management;
- Provides an 'institutionalized' accountability structure for management;
- Guards against self-serving conduct by the CEO; and
- Serves as an organizational 'safety net' for management of critical events or transitional phases.

1.1.5   What's in it for me?

In a healthy democracy, board membership provides an important opportunity for engaging citizens and developing community leadership. Most people volunteer for nonprofit and public sector boards out of a desire to contribute to their communities, advance a particular cause, or develop new skills or networks. Some people use their service on community boards to enhance their resumes or advance their political careers. Others join to 'do good works' and may not understand good governance or even be interested in providing it. Instead, to the consternation of management, staff and other board members, they often seek opportunities to become involved in the operational detail of the organization. Still others join to advance specific personal or political agendas and often become disruptive influences.

Motivation for serving on a board plays an important role in determining how well members of a board work together as a team and how effective they are in their role. There is evidence to support the common-sense notion that enthusiasm for the work of the organization, measured by the time board members commit to the organization, their engagement in strategic planning[16] and their commitment to the common cause or mission of the organization, is an important factor in effective board performance.[17] This requires that personal and political agendas be set aside and that board members focus on providing stewardship that is in the best interest of the organization they wish to serve. Having board members sign a letter of agreement can help you to ensure that they understand the organization's expectations of them and what they can expect from the organization. (See Part 8.3 for a sample letter of agreement for board members.)

> **Quick Tip**
>
> A nominations process that includes rigorous screening of the motivations of prospective board candidates will increase the prospect of recruiting people who will be a good fit for your organization and board. It will also reduce the likelihood of bringing on new board members who are primarily interested in their own agendas.

1.1.6   For-profit or not?

A for-profit organization is a legal corporation established for the purpose of making a profit for its shareholders (owners). Profit is typically thought of in financial terms, i.e., the amount of money earned by the business that is left after paying all expenses. Profit is the financial dividend to shareholders or return on their investment in the business enterprise. It is also the primary driver of most 'for-profit' corporations. The corporation's success is measured by return on investment and by net profit or loss on operations. However, the most successful and 'visionary' companies are "equally guided by a core ideology – core values and a sense of purpose beyond just making money."[18]

A nonprofit organization is "an organization that serves a public benefit (*or membership interest*), depends on volunteers at least for its governance, has limited direct control by government, other than in relation to tax benefits, and is not profit-making, thus eligible for exemption from paying income taxes."[19] A nonprofit organization, unlike its private sector counterpart, does not have the right to distribute profits or assets to shareholders (since no one can own 'shares' in a nonprofit) or confer other direct personal benefits upon its directors or members. Its 'owners' are the members of the corporation. Its primary driver is non-monetary, and is encapsulated in its mission and value statements, which typically speak about the public good or the membership benefits that the organization seeks to achieve. Because they are non-monetary, the benefits of a nonprofit organization are comparatively difficult to measure, particularly in 'softer' services such as health promotion, community development, arts and culture.

The purpose of an organization, as expressed in its letters patent or articles of incorporation, and the need for charitable status to support its objectives, will determine whether the organization is best constituted as a nonprofit or a for-profit corporation.

1.2   ESSENTIAL GOVERNANCE TASKS OF THE BOARD

All boards of directors, regardless of the type or size of the organization in question, have the same basic tasks.* The extent to which responsibility for these tasks is formalized in writing and/or the degree to which they are relevant to a particular organization will depend on the size and complexity of the organization and the resources available to support the board in its work. These tasks are to:

- **define** and/or safeguard the **mission**, the **values framework and operating principles** within which it expects the organization to be administered, and to review and update these periodically to ensure that they remain current and responsive;
- **oversee** development and approval of a **longer-term organizational plan or strategic priorities** and develop or approve annual budgets and operating plans;
- **monitor performance** of the organization overall **in relation to achievement of** its **mission, strategic goals and objectives**;
- **seek or secure sufficient resources** for the organization to adequately finance its operational and capital requirements;
- **account to members**, financial investors, other key stakeholders and the public **for the services** of the organization **and expenditure of funds**;
- **ensure prudent** and proper **management** of the organization's resources;
- **anticipate, mitigate and manage risks** to the organization, its staff, board, owners, clients and other key stakeholders;
- **establish** the general **values framework** within which the organization's **human resources** will be managed and periodically **monitor** key human resource **performance indicators**;
- **approve** and periodically review **personnel policies** within which human resources will be managed;
- **approve a mandate** (upper financial limits) within which **pay and benefits** agreements with staff (if there are any) are to be negotiated;
- **regularly review** the organization's **services** to ensure that they are consistent with the purpose of the organization and that its programs are effective and relevant to community needs;
- **provide continuity/stability** for the organization. Preserve the corporate memory;

---

* The primary stewardship and governance obligations of a board of directors to the organization's members, funders and the public are discussed in more detail in Part Three.

- **provide opportunities for** citizen **stakeholder** (shareholder) **participation**;
- **represent the organization** and its programs **positively** to key stakeholders and the community at large. **Be a good ambassador;**
- **serve as an advocate** for services of good quality; and
- **ensure fair arbitration of complaints** from consumers about services or products through a formal complaints procedure.

The following additional governance responsibilities apply to boards with an executive director or chief executive officer:

- **govern** the organization **through** broad **policies and planned objectives** approved by the board, formulated with the executive director and staff, and reviewed periodically;
- **select and support an executive director** to whom the responsibility for administration of the organization is delegated;
- **regularly review and evaluate** the **performance of the executive director** on the basis of a specific job description and negotiated performance objectives;
- **provide advice** and **act as a resource** and sounding board for the executive director or senior staff person; and
- **maintain sufficient independence from management and adequate knowledge** about the organization to ensure that the board can make reasonably objective judgements about the reliability and validity of management reports on finances and general operations.

1.3   DUTIES OF INDIVIDUAL DIRECTORS: WHAT'S EXPECTED OF ME?

Individual board members have no authority to act independently of the board except insofar as the bylaw or the board, by resolution, specifically mandates them to. This means, among other things, that an individual board member cannot provide direction to the executive director or staff. The only legal authority to provide direction or require information is vested in the full board.

Each board member is expected to become an active participant in a body that functions effectively as a whole. The sample letter of agreement in Part 8.3 provides a format for clearly laying out expectations. In addition to assisting in the fulfilment of the governance responsibilities noted earlier (see Part 1.2: Essential governance tasks of the board), board members must exercise due diligence, loyalty and care in the performance of their duties. Each board member is responsible to exercise these duties[20] as follows:

1.3.1 Duty of due diligence

- **Be informed** of the articles of incorporation (or letters patent), the legislation under which the organization exists, and the organization's bylaws, mission, values, code of conduct, and policies as they pertain to the duties of a director.
- **Keep generally informed** about the activities of the organization, the community issues that affect the organization and general trends in the business in which the organization operates.
- **Attend** board **meetings** regularly, serve on **committees** of the board and **contribute from** personal, professional and life **experience** to the work of the board.

1.3.2 Duty of loyalty

- **Act with honesty and in good faith in** what the director reasonably believes to be **the best interests of the corporation**.
- **Maintain solidarity** with fellow directors in support of a decision that has been made in good faith, in a legally constituted meeting, by directors in reasonably full possession of the facts.
- **Exercise vigilance for and declare** any apparent or real personal **conflict of interest** in accordance with the organization's bylaws and policies and statutory requirements.

1.3.3 Duty of care

- **Exercise** the same degree of **care, diligence and skill** that a **reasonably prudent person** would show in comparable circumstances. This may require a reasonable understanding of relevant legislation and jurisprudence.
- **Offer personal perspectives** and opinions on issues that are the subject of board discussion and decision.
- **Voice, clearly and explicitly,** at the time a decision is being taken, **any opposition to a decision being considered by the board**.
- **Ask for a review of a decision**, if the director has reasonable grounds to believe that the board acted without full information or in a manner inconsistent with its fiduciary obligations; if still not satisfied after such review, ask that the matter be placed before the membership or appointing body.
- **Work cooperatively with the staff** of the organization on committees or task forces of the board.
- **Know and respect the distinction in the roles of board and staff** consistent with the principles underlying approved governance policies.

Additional duties of members of fundraising (foundation) boards

- **Make personal financial commitments; secure** financial **commitments** from personal and business associates and/or **facilitate access** to those associates by other volunteers or fundraising staff.
- **Organize** and/or **participate** in **fundraising events** and **campaigns**.
- **Allocate**, or oversee the allocation or distribution of, **fundraising proceeds** in a manner consistent with the purposes for which they were raised.

1.4   LIABILITIES OF BOARD MEMBERS

Directors of nonprofit organizations often express concern about their personal liability. Many do not have enough information on the subject. Simply put, the duties and liabilities of directors arise from the organization's founding, or governing, documents, i.e., its constitution (articles of incorporation or letters patent), its bylaws and policies; the statute under which it was incorporated; various provincial/state or federal statutes; and the common law.

Statutory liabilities

Statutory liabilities may arise from failure of the organization to comply with the requirements of the legislation under which it is incorporated (hence the importance of knowing which statute is concerned), and/or the requirements of other applicable statutes (e.g., *Income Tax Act, Charities Accounting Act, Employment Insurance Act, Canada Pension Plan Act, Canadian Environmental Protection Act, Anti-terrorism Act, Privacy Act, etc.*).

Recent reviews suggest that there are approximately 200 sections under federal and provincial statutes in Canada that impose liability on directors or officers of a corporation located in Ontario. It appears that directors of nonprofits in Canada face the same liabilities (and penalties) as directors of business corporations, regardless of the size of the organization they serve and whether or not it has charitable status. Many jurisdictions in the United States have 'Good Samaritan' laws that protect those engaged in voluntary service on behalf of charitable causes, including directors, from many liabilities faced by for-profit directors. Legislation governing incorporation in some Canadian jurisdictions may also provide a statutory defense to personal claims against directors who have acted in good faith, with due diligence. See proposed Canada Not-for-Profit Corporations Act.

Common law liabilities

Common law liabilities may arise when directors act outside of the scope of authority provided in the corporation's governing documents.

The following are some of the most common causes of personal liability for board members:

- Directors **sign contracts** on behalf of the organization without proper authorization from the board. The bylaws should provide specific authority for directors and officers to execute legal documents.
- Directors commit **tortious acts** such as negligent mismanagement or careless oversight causing injury. This "relates to situations where the board knew of, or ought to have foreseen, a systemic problem and failed to address it."
- Directors **breach their fiduciary duty**, i.e., "the corporation suffers a loss that can be directly attributed to their actions or omissions" in the proper exercise of their duties. In *Public Guardian and Trustee v. Aids Society for Children,* an application under Ontario's *Charities Accounting Act*, it was held that directors could be held personally liable if funds are not used in accordance with representations made when the funds were collected.
- Directors **breach their trustee duties**. This includes use of funds or property other than for the purposes intended by funders or donors, improper investment of funds and remuneration of directors other than for personal expenses incurred in relation to their director's duties. Charitable corporations are held to a higher standard in this regard than nonprofits without charitable status.
- **Employee and workplace liability.** Among other things, directors are held responsible for "all debts owed to employees of the corporation for services provided for the corporation." The liability is joint and several, which means each director is personally liable for the full amount, e.g., *up to* six months' wages, guaranteed bonuses and vacation pay, in the case of Ontario.

Directors who conscientiously fulfill the duties of due diligence, loyalty and care outlined above can manage or minimize most of the risks, or liabilities, to which they might otherwise be exposed. Additional safeguards include:

- a bylaw clause indemnifying directors from liabilities arising from their actions or omissions as directors provided that they have exercised their duties with due diligence and care (note: indemnification is meaningful only if the organization has the funds to back it up at the precise moment that the director requires protection);
- D&O (directors' and officers') liability insurance, available to boards that decide that the size, complexity or scope of the organization warrant the extra protection (and cost);
- arranging for members of the organization, during its annual general meeting, to ratify the directors' acts;
- drafting bylaws in the broadest possible terms so that the directors have the authority to engage in a wide range of activities;

- seeking written opinions from qualified experts on matters beyond the competence of the board (including legal advice on specific liabilities affecting the board); and
- ensuring that appropriate controls are in place for issuing and signing checks, contracts, tax receipts, etc.

Although, in reality, most directors of nonprofit organizations have little to fear, the liabilities to which they are potentially subject may be so daunting that they serve as a real disincentive to membership on a volunteer board. Prospective directors should be told that there are very few cases on record in which directors of nonprofits have actually been subjected to financial penalties. Nevertheless, it is also advisable to be as straightforward as possible about liability issues when recruiting new board members, and to make sure that the board as a whole is well informed on the subject. Boards should also be aware that the legal liability landscape is far from static.

For more details on directors' duties and liabilities in Canada, see *Primer for Directors of Not-for-Profit Corporations: Rights, Duties, and Practices,* [21] which is the primary source for much of the overview of directors' duties and liabilities found in Parts 1.3 and 1.4.

1.5   THE GOOD GOVERNANCE/GOOD MANAGEMENT PARTNERSHIP

It is important to note that the distinctions made here between governance and management refer to functions, not to who performs them. For example, members of operational and management boards (and, in some instances, collective boards) perform both governance and management functions. Members of operational boards also perform work that would normally be undertaken by staff in larger organizations. (See Part 1.1.3 for discussion of the basic organizational functions and Part 2.2 and Appendix A for discussion of board types.)

Good governance is both about achieving desired results and achieving them in the right way; that is, in a way that is consistent with the values of democracy and social justice (see Figure 2). This is particularly important in the voluntary sector where values typically play an important role in determining both organizational purpose and style of operation. Good governance emerges through ethical application of prevailing laws and organizational norms or traditions, and respect for the spirit behind these.

Good governance involves:

- *vision, values and vigilance* (envisioning the future, providing the values foundation for the organization, and overseeing its operations);
- *participation* (involving key stakeholders in planning);
- *destination, direction and decisions* (setting goals, providing a general 'road

map' and making clear and timely decisions);

- *transparency* (in decision making and operations);
- *resources* (securing the resources necessary to achieve the goals of the organization or reach its destination without undue risks to stakeholders);
- *monitoring performance* (periodically ensuring that the organization is well-maintained and progressing, within legal limits, toward its destination); and
- *accountability* (ensuring efficient use of resources; reporting progress and detours to stakeholders).

Management, by classical definition, is 'getting things done through people'. It is the *organization of tasks, people, relationships, resources and technology to achieve the organizational purpose* (see Figure 3). If we picture the organization as a bus or ship, then the function of management is to steer the (organizational) vehicle or vessel toward the destination set by the board; influence and implement decisions of the board; know the road map or navigational routes, examine alternate routes and select the course; ensure efficient resource consumption and good maintenance of the (organizational) vehicle or vessel; regularly assess progress and travel conditions; adjust course when advisable; and provide periodic travel reports to the board, crew and passengers.

Governance and management are sound when good strategic decisions are made, clear and transparent accountability provisions exist, available resources are used effectively, organizational norms are respected in both policies and operations, appropriate relationships prevail with stakeholders and community, and the organization proves capable of adapting over time. With good governance and good management, the organization can achieve its objectives, remain financially viable and be credible in the eyes of its stakeholders.

Figures 2 and 3 provide a brief comparison of these functions.

Figure 2: Good governance

Good governance: Providing a framework

- Vision, Values and Vigilance
- Participation
- Destination/Direction & Decisions
- Transparency
- Resources
- Monitoring Performance
- Accountability

Figure 3: Good management

Good management: Implementing within the framework

- Knowing the map/resources/conditions
- Selecting a course from alternate routes
- Steering toward destination
- Ensuring efficient use of resources and good maintenance of the organization
- Assessing progress and conditions
- Reporting to board, crew and passengers

Quick Tip
– Meddlesome board members

Beware the board member or chair that has a propensity to meddle or who has excessive amounts of time to devote to an organization in which management has been delegated to a CEO.

Such individuals often tend to transgress the boundaries between governance and management. A chair who meddles in management can seriously impair both board and CEO accountability, and confuse staff and other stakeholders.

To produce maximum value for the organization, governance and management must be a true partnership. Although board members typically have limited time to devote to the organization's affairs, they can provide an objective perspective by linking the organization to key stakeholders and the community. CEOs, on the other hand, work at the job full time and have intimate knowledge, information and expertise that board members simply cannot be expected to possess. CEOs also, perhaps inevitably, have a much greater degree of personal investment (emotional and reputational) in the organization than do most board members.

Within this partnership, however, the respective roles of the board and the CEO should be articulated as clearly as possible and disagreements or conflicts about where the role of the board ends and that of the CEO begins should be constructively and promptly resolved.

Case Illustration – Blurred boundaries between board and staff

A majority of the members of the board of the York Children's Aid Society resigned in April 1991 because of conflicts with the Ministry of Community and Social Services over funding that did not keep pace with the increase in demand for service and the growing population in the region. Following the board walkout, the Ministry invoked its power to manage the agency and appointed a newly incorporated body, the Children and Family Services for York Region, to operate the agency on the Ministry's behalf.

The board chair, having ample time on his hands during a period of serious trouble for the agency, interpreted the Ministry's charge to manage the agency literally. He took up an office on site and designated himself 'Chief Executive Officer'. This blurring of boundaries between policy-making and management functions resulted in a frequent turnover of the staff CEOs and significant lack of trust among staff in the leadership of the board.

Between 1991 and 1999, five 'permanent' or interim CEOs graced the corner office. This was in large measure due to the lack of clear role and boundary definitions between board (governance) and executive (management) functions.

PART TWO – FROM GOVERNANCE MODELS TO BEST PRACTICE BENCHMARKS

The preoccupation with the Carver 'policy governance' model[22] over the past decade has left many organizations wondering about the legitimacy of alternative approaches to governance and frustrated with the lack of a coherent framework for determining which approach might be most suitable for their particular organization. (An overview of the policy governance model is provided in Parts 2.2, 2.3 and Appendix A.)

My research led me to conclude that alternatives to the Carver 'one size fits all' policy governance model are not broadly known, nor does a coherent framework exist that would help organizations decide which approach to use. During 2000-2001 I conducted in-depth case studies on the governance practices of 20 nonprofit and public sector organizations[23] across Canada to identify commonly used governance models and the factors that influenced their approach to governance. The case studies assessed the finances and governance practices of the 20 organizations over a ten-year period through a review of key documents, interviews with senior staff and board members and analysis of responses to the Governance Self-Assessment Checklist.[24] The 20 organizations studied were from several nonprofit sectors ranging from a small rural service club with no operating budget to education and health boards with budgets well into the millions of dollars. The median budget size was approximately $3,000,000.

The research initially defined a governance model as 'a distinctive set or cluster of governance *structures*, *responsibilities* (functions) and *practices* (processes) that are logically consistent with one another, have a high degree of internal coherence and are bound together by values or by assumptions about good governance practices.' Structure refers to the *parameters for selection and operation* of the board established by legislation, regulations, bylaws and policies. Responsibilities refers to *what functions* boards are expected to perform. Practices (processes) refers to *how* those governance *functions are exercised*.

I found that approaches to governance vary according to how a board is structured and how responsibilities are distributed among board, management and staff. It also varies in the processes used for board development, management and decision-making. The factors that most influence the approach that a board takes or ought to take to the way it organizes and fulfills its governance responsibilities are the legislative and regulatory context of the nonprofit organization, its ownership as defined by how the board is selected, the requirement for accountability to key stakeholder constituencies, and its mandate and funding.

2.1   FROM GOVERNANCE MODELS TO BOARD TYPES

Voluntary organizations and their boards may be classified in a variety of ways, e.g., by the purpose, life or developmental cycle of the organization;[25] size, age, sector, legal status or organizational form (e.g., charitable, incorporated or unincorporated); legal mandate (established by legislation other than incorporation legislation to serve a particular public purpose such as hospitals, schools, universities, child welfare agencies, crown corporations); and ownership structure (i.e., the process used to select the board).

While there may be a fine distinction between board types and governance models, I have concluded that the concept of a board type is more useful than the concept of governance model. Board types are categorized here according to their primary purpose and activities. The key characteristics of the nine board types identified through this research are described below (see Table 1). While all incorporated boards have governance responsibilities, the typology of boards offered here is based on the primary focus of board attention and activities.

2.2   OVERVIEW OF BOARD TYPES

The board types described here range from those that are heavily involved in operations (usually in small organizations with little or no staff) to those with little or no operational involvement (usually in larger organizations with an executive director or chief executive officer). They differ in the degree of involvement in operations and the distribution of responsibilities and decision-making power as well as in their primary focus. They may also differ in how members are selected and their use of committees. It is important to note that these board types are descriptive rather than prescriptive, and that their characteristics are not always mutually exclusive. Many boards are hybrids that draw on two or more of these types.

For example, the success of smaller organizations may depend largely or entirely on board involvement in management or staff functions, while the complexity of larger organizations, many with professional mandates, makes such direct 'hands-on' involvement by board members inadvisable. Local organizations are usually more directly accessible to board members and allow for more frequent meetings and a closer proximity to operations. Geographic distance (and budgets) may limit the frequency of board and committee meetings in provincial/ state or national organizations, which in turn may limit direct involvement in 'staff' work.

Table 1 – Board types based on primary board focus

1. **Operational (primary focus: operations)** – The board does the work of the organization and manages as well as governs it. This is typical of a board in the 'founding' stage of an organization and of boards in organizations, such as service clubs, that have no staff and that must rely largely on board members and other volunteers to achieve their aims. Operational boards also have management responsibilities but are distinguished from management boards by their lack of staff support.

2. **Collective (primary focus: operations/inclusive decision-making processes)** – The board and staff are involved in 'single team' decision-making about governance and the work of the organization. Board members may be involved in some of the service or management functions. Staff leaders have strong influence on governance and may, in fact, dominate decision-making. Boards of collectives with no staff are operational boards that govern on the basis of specific values related to decision-making.

3. **Management (primary focus: management of operations)** – The board manages operations but may have a staff coordinator. Board members actively manage finances, personnel and service delivery directly or as committee chairs and report directly to the board. Staff reports to board member managers either directly or through a dual reporting line to a board member and a staff coordinator.

4. **Constituent representational (primary focus: constituent interests)** – An approach used by publicly elected bodies, federations or other constituency-elected boards whose primary responsibility is to balance the best interests of the overall organization against the interests of its constituents. Members of such boards often find it difficult to achieve this balance and are sometimes pressured to favor constituent interests. They may, as in the case of publicly elected bodies, carry grievance resolution/ombudsman functions and may consequently be drawn inappropriately into operational matters to solve constituent problems. They may also, as in the case of some school boards, have prescribed responsibilities for public consultation and human resources. This approach to governance may also be an element of other board types.

5. **Traditional (primary focus: governance)** – The board governs and oversees operations through committees but delegates management functions to the CEO. Committees, established along functional lines (e.g., finance, human resources, programs) that parallel management functions, are used to process information for the board and sometimes do the work of the board. The

committee structure and ambiguity in roles may invite board interference in management functions. The CEO may have a primary reporting relationship to the board through the chair.

6. **Results-based (primary focus: governance)** – This type of board is focused on setting a clear direction for the organization and getting the best results for the money invested. The CEO is a non-voting member of the board, carries substantial influence over policy-making and direction, is viewed as a full partner with the board and has a relatively free hand at managing to achieve objectives established by the board. Committees are used for monitoring/auditing the performance of the board, CEO and organization. Board members are selected for community representativeness and commitment to the organization's purpose, and may be used for selected tasks in their area of expertise.

7. **Policy governance (primary focus: governance)** – The board governs through policies that establish organizational aims ("ends"); governance approaches or processes; management limitations; and that define the board/CEO relationship. The CEO has broad freedom to determine the "means" that will be implemented to achieve organizational aims. The CEO reports to the full board. The board does not use committees but may use task teams to assist it in specific aspects of its work.

8. **Fundraising board (primary focus: fundraising activities)** –These boards, more commonly referred to as 'foundations' in Canada, are incorporated separately and at varying degrees of 'arm's-length' from their beneficiary charities. While they have responsibility for the governance of the organization, their primary focus is on raising funds to support charitable causes. They are, in this sense, operational in nature although they may have staff to support and coordinate their activities. Members become directly involved in various aspects of fundraising. Their governance function is focused on setting direction and strategies and providing general oversight of staff activities, finances and allocations. This type of board may also be operational if the organization has no staff; management if it has few staff; or more focused on governance if it has a substantial staff complement. In any case, its primary focus is fundraising.

9. **Advisory board (primary focus: advice and connections)** – This type of board is typically selected and dominated by the CEO. It provides prima facie legitimacy to the organization but governs only in a nominal sense. Board members are selected for profile and contacts that will lend credibility to the organization and facilitate access to funding. Essentially, an advisory board provides advice and rubber-stamps CEO-recommended budget and plans. It should not be confused with an advisory 'committee', which has no decision-making authority.

Figure 4 shows the degree of board member involvement in 'operations' or the actual 'staff' work of the organization relative to the organization's geographic scope or jurisdiction (local, provincial/state or national), the size of its budget/staff and the complexity of its operations, as discovered in my research. Note that constituent representational and fundraising board structures and practices tend to overlap with other board types and cut across jurisdictional lines.

Figure 4: Board involvement in operations relative to the jurisdiction, size and complexity of the organization

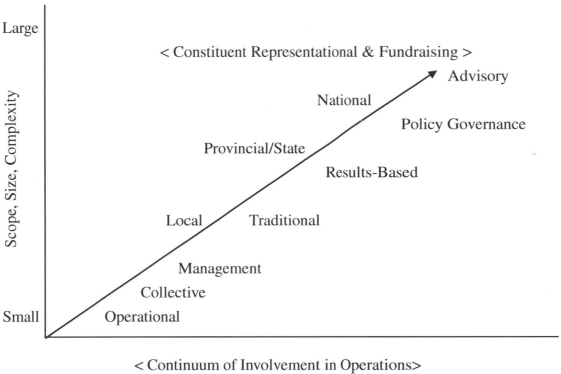

Generally, small, local organizations are more likely to have operational, collective and management types of boards that are heavily involved in operations. Large, complex, and sometimes national, organizations may lean toward boards that have policy governance or advisory characteristics.

While the traditional board type still appears to be the most common, my research revealed that many organizations use hybrid approaches that they create by applying practices from different board types to different aspects of their mission or primary responsibilities. For example, boards are more likely to delegate day-to-day service operations, human resources and financial management (as advocated by Carver's 'board ends/CEO means' distinction) than they are to delegate social policy development. They are more likely to take a 'hands-on' or 'operational' approach to advocacy, fundraising and crisis management. While this clearly indicates a dynamic process for governance design, this mix-and-match approach is often adopted without a systematic rationale and doesn't necessarily serve the best interests of the organization.

Subsequent research using the Governance Self-Assessment Checklist[26] with 32 additional nonprofits found *no significant difference in either board or organizational effectiveness based on the governance model (or board type) employed*. This is generally consistent with the conclusions of a recent study on the policy governance model that the particular approach to governance generally mattered less than the fact that a board was paying serious attention to its governance practices with a view to self-improvement.[27]

Figure 5 provides another perspective on this typology organized around the primary focus of the various board types. Again the constituent representational dynamic and fundraising requirement may be elements within other board types and have varying degrees of operational involvement. Similarly, Operational, Collective and Management Boards may adopt aspects of any of the board types whose primary focus is governance to create a unique hybrid approach to governance that best suits their organizational values, purposes and context.

Figure 5: Board types by primary focus

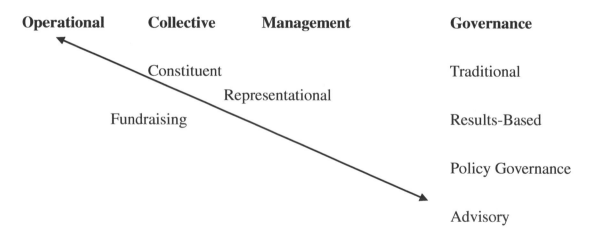

Another way to understand the differences between board types is to examine who – board or staff – is responsible for the three key functions of the organization – governance, management, and work or operations. Table 2 provides a comparison of the board types based on responsibility for these functions.

Table 2 - Distribution of Responsibilities and Decision-making Power

Board Type	Governance	Management	Work
Operational	Board	Board	Board
Collective	Board/Staff	Staff/Board	Staff/Board
Management	Board	Board	Staff
Constituent Representational	Board	Board/CEO	Staff
Traditional	CEO/Board*	CEO/Board**	Staff
Results-Based	Board/CEO partnership	CEO	Staff
Policy Governance	Board	CEO	Staff
Advisory	CEO/Board***	CEO	Staff
Fundraising	Board/CEO	CEO/Board	Staff/Board

* Traditional boards often have CEO-dominant leadership during normal times. The board is more likely to dominate during times of crisis, particularly in the event of a precipitous departure of the CEO.

** Traditional boards typically structure committees to oversee key management functions. This often leads board members to be drawn into areas of management and to second-guess management decisions or to 'micro-manage'.

*** Governance by advisory (rubber-stamp) boards is typically CEO-dominated. As noted elsewhere, this is a board type that has abrogated its governance functions, has high liability risks and is not recommended.

Each organization has its own culture and unique set of circumstances. These must be taken into consideration when designing a governance structure and system that will work best for any given organization. The first step in selecting the right governance structure is to understand how the concepts of governance should be applied to the organization in question. My case studies revealed that "determination of an approach to governance that's right for a particular organization clearly requires more than selection from a menu of available alternatives. It requires a creative application of practical knowledge and a basic understanding of how various concepts of governance fit their particular organization."[28]

The most important factors to consider when deciding on an organization's approach to governance (and the desired degree of board involvement in operations or management) appear, from my research,[29] to be:

- past practice;
- the size and complexity of the organization;
- the organization's 'ownership' structure;
- transitional phases in organizational development;
- the timing and nature of critical events; and
- the personal or political agendas of board members.

These don't always come together in a way that supports effective organizational performance.

Quick Tip

Different developmental stages, transitional phases and critical events are likely to require different approaches to governance. Good governance practices are more important than theoretical governance models.

Case Illustration: A collective board

This Women's Addiction Treatment Service (Amethyst), founded in 1979, provides addiction treatment programs and education for women with alcohol and drug addiction problems. It operated with a budget of $630,000 in 1999.

It started its operations with a traditional governance model but evolved over time into a collective. This is the reverse of what might have been expected. Most boards tend to evolve from collectives into a more traditional type. The organization managed through crises of leadership, philosophy and financial viability over a decade. It continues to struggle with reconciling its 'feminist philosophy' and commitment to a collective organizational form with funder preferences for a single management contact person.

The Centre's approach to governance reflected a blend of the management and collective board types. Board members and staff shared responsibilities for key management functions such as financial management, program supervision, staff selection and evaluation. It had, however, retained strong elements of a collective model: consensus decision making; shared values about organizational purpose; group accountability for group decisions; salary parity among staff; rigorous group screening of new board members; and strongly inclusive group dynamics with mutual support for personal concerns. The perception of board members was that the organization most closely resembled a collective (staff-owned) model.

The legal 'owners' of Amethyst are its approximately 100 members who have a particular interest in Amethyst's work. The general membership supports Amethyst through participation in committees, fundraising, financial contributions and promoting community awareness of the organization. The board is also accountable to funders for the overall administration of the Centre's grants.

Operational, collective and management boards may work well for smaller organizations, but they are generally inappropriate for boards that have delegated responsibility for management to an executive director or staff coordinator and that have staff to perform vital operational tasks. The constituent representation board is a discreet type in itself, but its propensity to represent the organization's constituents may also appear in other board types. This can deflect directors from their responsibility to act in the overall best interests of the nonprofit they govern. The advisory type of board is fraught with risks to the personal liability of directors and the organization itself. Others have referred to this as a 'rubber-stamp' board. None of these approaches – operational, collective, management, constituent representational or advisory – is recommended for the typical mid-sized or larger nonprofit. Moreover, regardless of board type, directors are well advised to pay attention to governance basics and maintain a focus on the results sought for their organizations.

Mid-sized and larger nonprofits are typically left with three choices: a traditional governance approach, a results-based approach, or a policy governance approach.

> **Quick Tip**
>
> Some statutes governing incorporation, such as the Canada Corporations Act, specifically charge directors to act in the overall best interests of the corporation. It's a good idea to write this provision into your bylaws and reinforce it in your governance policies.

2.3 A WORD ABOUT THE POLICY GOVERNANCE MODEL

John Carver vaulted to fame as a 'governance guru' in the early 1990s with the publication and promotion of his 'policy governance' model.[30] Private, public and voluntary sector boards across North America have tried, with varied degrees of success, to implement this model or adapt it to their own organization's needs and context. Many have expressed frustration, saying that it is too complex to understand and implement, requires too much time and training, creates too much distance between the board and organization and erodes board control and accountability. Carver, in response, maintains that his model is suited to any type of organization and will benefit those in which it is properly (i.e., fully) implemented.

However, "The obligation of directors of not-for-profit corporations to oversee the operation of the corporation and ensure compliance with the corporation's objects is an onerous one. Some models of board governance, such as Carver's, advocate that directors limit themselves to policy matters only and leave responsibility for administration and day-to-day matters with the executive staff of the corporation."[31] Such limitation on the role of directors does not absolve them of their obligations under Canadian law to properly report and account for the operation of the organization.

On the one hand, there is general consensus that the promotion of the 'Carver model' has usefully focused attention on governance generally. Many of its elements have been particularly enlightening for the boards that have adopted or adapted this model, particularly the 'board-ends and management-means' distinction, the board focus on policy rather than operational matters, the importance of board solidarity (speaking with one voice), the CEO as a board's only employee, and the clear line of accountability from staff to the CEO and from the CEO to the 'whole board'. It has contributed as well to the general discourse on governance.

On the other hand, there has been significant concern that promotion of a 'one size fits all' model, rigorously applied, has drawn attention away from alternative models that may be more suitable for many voluntary organizations. This is especially true of smaller organizations where relationships among the board, staff, volunteers and consumers may need to be more collaborative. Indeed, such collaboration is increasingly recognized as a key factor in the success of any organization.

Carver's proposition that the board should conduct its work largely independent of the CEO creates serious structural tensions. Chief among these is the 'principal-agent' paradox in which the board bears legal responsibility for the organization but does not, in many if not most cases, have the same knowledge, resources or time as the executive director and staff to be able to plan and direct the organization or monitor its performance independently.[32]

The debate about the policy governance model was an important backdrop to my decision to search for alternative governance models or board types, and to place these within a coherent framework that would allow boards to decide which governance approach might be more, or most, appropriate for their organization.

2.4   SELECTING THE RIGHT APPROACH: BOARD TYPES OR BEST PRACTICES?

Most of the boards that I studied in my research evolved into a dynamic 'hybrid' of several board types. In one case, the board and staff shared operational responsibility for development of public policy positions, public education and policy promotion while respecting the Carver 'ends/means' distinction in the areas of finances, human resources and program administration.

In other cases, the board was active in collective bargaining and personnel selection, which in larger organizations is typically left to management.

Many of the traditional boards that I studied experienced problems because they had made no clear demarcation between governance and management roles. Many had a committee structure that paralleled management and operational functions (e.g., finance committee, human resources committee, programs committee, public relations committee, etc.). This inevitably invites board intrusion into operational detail. Meeting agendas typically mimicked this structure. Focusing on management and operations instead of on results impairs the ability of governing boards to 'add value' to the organization and to account meaningfully to key stakeholders.

The results-based approach to governance is a 'hybrid' approach that is emerging in some leading edge nonprofits.[33] It addresses weaknesses identified in other approaches through a judicious use of committees structured around board, rather than management, responsibilities. The executive committee (poorly used in many nonprofits) carries responsibility for leading strategic planning and evaluating CEO performance. A governance committee is responsible for regular review of bylaws, governance policies and practices as well as board (member) recruitment, development and evaluation. Risk management and quality audit committees ensure mitigation of risk, establish clear measures of organizational performance in key areas, monitor and audit performance, and report on results. The 'board-ends and management-means' distinction is maintained for the general management of finances, human resources and program operations. Table 3 compares the three board types that have a primary focus on governance.

Table 3 – Comparison of three board types with a primary focus on governance

	Traditional	**Policy Governance**	**Results-Based**
General Focus	*Operations/event driven*	*Policies driven: ends and governance processes*	*Vision/results driven*
Leadership	*CEO dominant – chair is link to board; executive committee comprises core group*	*Board ends/CEO means*	*Full board/CEO partnership to set direction and expected results; Executive committee members act as core advisors*
Planning	*CEO leads; committees vet; board reviews and approves*	*Board ends/CEO means*	*CEO leads; board, actively engaged, links organization to community*
Committees	*Parallel management functions*	*Ad hoc task forces*	*Based on board responsibilities*
Accountability	*CEO dominant in reporting to key stakeholders; board nominally responsible*	*CEO reports to full board, which monitors policy compliance and reports to owners*	*Board dominant: sets direction, monitors, audits and reports on results* *CEO reports to full board*

The results-based board (sometimes referred to as an audit/oversight board) is distinct from the policy governance board in four key ways:

1. The CEO is a non-voting member of the board with full entitlement to attend and participate in all meetings and discussions.
2. The CEO is a full partner with the board in direction and policy-making.
3. The board's general focus is on auditing results rather than on policy compliance.
4. The board uses 'standing committees' to guide, monitor and audit board, CEO and organizational performance.

Board members are selected for community representation and commitment to the organization's purpose, and may be used for selected tasks in their area of expertise. The board's focus is on mission, values, objectives, strategic planning, effectiveness in achieving goals and efficient use of resources. Board members are usually community members who have a significant personal interest in the 'public benefits' of the organization.

Although the results-based board monitors performance, it is not involved in day-to-day operations. It is similar to a policy governance board in this sense and in its focus on organizational 'ends'.

Committees used for monitoring and auditing the performance of the board, CEO and organization typically include an executive committee, a governance committee, an audit or risk management committee and a quality assurance or program audit committee.

The results-based board differs from the traditional board in four key ways:

1. It uses committees to do the board's work rather than to review management activities.
2. The general focus of the board is on governance responsibilities rather than on management or operational matters.
3. The general focus of the board is on results (i.e., input efficiency, outputs and outcomes).
4. There is a full partnership between the board and CEO; neither the board nor the CEO dominates the relationship.

No single approach to governance has proven suitable for every organization. The factors discussed above are important considerations both in understanding what drives boards to adopt certain practices and what practices might be appropriate for a particular organization at a particular stage of its evolution. General insights can be derived from an analysis of the strengths and weaknesses of specific board types. But no matter which approach an organization uses, if it is to be effective, it must be adapted to the specific circumstances of the organization. Moreover, trust, mutual respect, honest communications and collaborative relationships are essential to the board/CEO partnership, regardless of formal structures and policies.

> ### Case Illustration: Board/CEO partnership helps an organization weather change
>
> Kinark Child and Family Services is a fully accredited, nonprofit children's mental health center that provides a range of mental health services for children up to the age of 18 and to their families. It operates with a volunteer board that represents multiple stakeholders including people from various regional communities and service consumers. Its operating budget was $17.4 million in 1999.
>
> Kinark's governance had been highly successful over the previous 10 years. It managed to keep clients' needs central and to adapt its mission and programs to a changing social and funding environment. It transformed itself from an agency in danger of being shut down by its funding Ministry, due to lack of productivity, to an influential and successful organization guided by objectives, benchmarks and evaluation of results. It actively pursued new revenue sources to compensate for cuts to its base funding in the mid-1990s and remained open to innovative business models and partnerships.
>
> A strong working partnership between the board and CEO was key to providing the strong, steady leadership needed to implement massive organizational change. The degree of change took its toll and led to organizational fatigue. The board and CEO needed the staff to make huge changes in how they viewed and performed their roles. The organization's more business-like approach, which involved greater accountability for results, did not initially resonate well with a staff steeped in a human services values set. The board and a new executive director agreed to slow the pace of change to deal with the 'change overload' felt by front line workers.
>
> The board was composed of high profile, credible members who adopted governance practices and a committee structure that are best characterized as results-based combined with elements of both traditional and policy governance approaches.

It is becoming increasingly apparent that there are certain governance 'best' or 'recommended' practices that cut across 'governance models' or 'board types' and that adoption or adaptation of these to particular organizational circumstances is more important than debate about which theoretical model a board should employ. The discussion in the remainder of this guide will help you to fulfill the responsibilities of your board and to decide which governance structures and practices are best suited to your board and organization.

PART THREE – BOARD RESPONSIBILITIES

SEVEN PRIMARY AREAS OF BOARD RESPONSIBILITY

The responsibilities of the board constitute 'the what of governance'. These responsibilities fall under seven general headings. They are:

- establishing and/or safeguarding the mission and planning for the future;
- financial stewardship;
- human resources stewardship;
- performance monitoring and accountability to key stakeholders;
- community representation, education and advocacy;
- risk management; and
- managing, or ensuring proper management of, 'critical events' and 'transitional phases'.

The board members and CEOs who participated in my research[34] identified their most significant weaknesses as human resources stewardship, risk management, performance monitoring, and mission and planning, in that order. Earlier research[35] also identified financial stewardship as an area of serious default.

> **Quick Tip**
>
> The essence of all board responsibilities is to set direction, monitor performance, audit results, keep an eye out for gathering storms and make sure the organization navigates safely through them.

3.1 ESTABLISHING/SAFEGUARDING THE MISSION AND PLANNING FOR THE FUTURE

Sound planning contributes to the development of a solid foundation for an organization. A fundamental premise of *Governing for Results* is that the responsibility for planning and direction of the organization is jointly shared in a full partnership between the board and CEO. The responsibility for expenditure of public funds creates an imperative to 'know where you're going' and to account for the results as well as for the costs and other consequences of the

A note on terminology

There is considerable confusion over planning terminology. Contradictory meanings are often attached to specific terms. In this book:

♦ strategic planning is used to mean development of a longer-term plan that outlines the organization's priorities and the direction it will take to achieve its mission and its most important goals and objectives;

♦ operational planning refers to the annual budget and operating plan developed as a management function and approved by the board; and

♦ tactics refers to the specific management measures that will be taken to implement the operational plan and progress toward achievement of the strategic plan.

journey. The essence of results-based planning and evaluation is captured in a paraphrase of a Zen conundrum:

"If you don't know where you're going, and you don't know where you're starting from, how will you know if or when you get there, or if you have made any progress at all?"

An essential prerequisite to effective planning and governance is to *know what business you're in*. The mandates of nonprofit organizations generally fall within one or more of eight primary purposes or 'missions'.

These are:

- service to the public or community (e.g., health care, general education, social services, recreation, sports, arts, culture, community associations, etc.);
- service to members (e.g., networking, training, research, advocacy, regulation, benefits, etc. Members may be professionals, individuals or organizations, including religious institutions.);
- research;
- education;
- policy development;
- advocacy;
- fundraising; and
- community development.

The organization's 'business' may require, or make it advisable for, a board to structure itself and exercise its responsibilities one way rather than another. For example, community associations may need a board committee to deal with community relations. A member services organization may see a need for a member services committee. A board engaged in fundraising may need board or committee involvement in planning events or allocating funds. An organization whose primary mandate is policy advocacy is likely to demand greater board involvement in that function and create committee structures and decision-making processes to support that function. However, the size, complexity and geographic scope of the organization are often more important in determining the structure the board will need and how it will exercise its responsibilities. (See 4.3: Organizing for accountable governance.)

In addition to knowing what business you're in, you need to know your organization. Specifically, you should:

- know its purpose, history, traditions and current organizational culture;
- understand the 'context' (financial, community and general environment) in which the organization operates;
- regularly scan the environment to determine relevant political, organizational and financial factors within which your organization operates; this includes an understanding of complementary and competing organizations;
- develop agreement among directors and other key stakeholders on a clear statement of the core values, mission and purpose of the organization to ensure that key players operate from a common base; and
- develop a long-term 'business' or corporate plan and clear benchmarks for measuring progress. This will increase the likelihood of achieving objectives.

It is the board's job to determine "what human needs are satisfied, for whom and at what cost."[36] A basic plan is essential to making this determination; for 'knowing where you're going, whether and/or when you get there'. Indeed, board engagement in the planning and direction of an organization is one of the variables that correlates most strongly with organizational effectiveness.[37]

> **Quick Tip**
>
> Creating an annual work plan for the board, distinct from, but complementary to, that of the organization, improves the chances that the board will 'add value' to the organization's efforts.

However, it is unwise to become perpetually 'stuck in the planning mode'. A Gallup study offers evidence that "Visionary companies make some of their best moves by experimentation, trial and error, opportunism, and – quite literally – accident. What looks in retrospect like brilliant foresight and preplanning was often the result of 'Let's just try a lot of stuff and keep what works.'"[38] This view is supported by Zimmerman, co-author of *Edgeware*,[39] who recommends "minimum specifications" in "a 'good enough vision'…simple documents that describe the general direction the organization is pursuing, and a few basic principles for how the organization gets there" and then allowing, within the strategic priorities established by the board, "appropriate autonomy for individuals (*those volunteers, management or staff responsible for implementation*) to self-organize and adapt as time goes by." Strategic planning can make the mistake of assuming, according to Henry Mintzberg, one of the world's leading experts on management and organizational behavior, that "the world is supposed to hold still while a formal plan is being developed and then stay on the predicted course while that plan is being implemented."[40]

None of these cautions negates the importance of the board's responsibility to at least provide a general direction for the organization and establish priorities that will help it advance toward its goals. The key is to continually review these priorities and adapt them to changing circumstances discovered through regular scanning of the organizational environment.

3.1.1   Vision, Mission and Values

Vision, mission and values form the cornerstone of sound planning.

A *vision* statement is a clear, succinct articulation of the desired future. It is a description, in broad, somewhat idealistic, terms, of the 'destination' that the organization strives to reach. Examples of vision statements are: 'eradication of child poverty', 'no child left behind', 'health care for all' or 'a clean, pure environment'.

The *mission* of an organization is its reason for existence, its 'cause', how it will contribute, at least in some measure, to its stated vision. The mission or purpose should be "a perpetual guiding star on the horizon: not to be confused with specific goals or business strategies."[41]

Values underpin vision and mission. "Core values are the organization's essential and enduring tenets – a small set of general guiding principles; not to be compromised for financial gain or short-term expediency."[42] Values establish the moral and ethical framework within which volunteers, managers and staff are expected to carry on their work.

Although planning purists suggest that vision, mission and values should be articulated separately, a mission statement can embody some elements of all three, as in the following example drawn from a child welfare agency[43]:

Our mission is: Within the legislative mandate and authority of the Child and Family Services Act; in cooperation with other agencies and the community; and with respect for the dignity and needs of the people we serve and those who provide the service:

♦ to provide the highest quality of service that is feasible to support families in caring for their children;

♦ to protect and, where necessary, ensure alternate care for children who may be neglected or abused or have other special needs; and

♦ to be an advocate for the well being of children and their families.

See Part 8.9 for a sample Values statement from this same organization.

Most newly recruited board members join organizations that already have an established mission statement. In such instances, the responsibility of the board is to safeguard that mission and ensure that it remains current and responsive to a changing environment. The mission should not, however, "sway with the trends and fads of the day" but should provide an anchor from which progress is driven.[44]

3.1.2   Goals, objectives and measurement benchmarks

Goals are more specific statements about the general purposes of the organization than are typically found in the mission statement. Establishment of goals is an essential component of providing clear direction for an organization. Use the following guide to assist you in getting the results you desire:

- Establish *goals* and a broad *strategy* to achieve them.
- Ensure that your organization establishes *SMART* objectives:
  - **S**pecific;
  - **M**easurable;
  - **A**chievable within the specified period;
  - **R**elevant to the organizational mission; and
  - **T**ime delineated.
- Delegate responsibility for implementation of the strategy and achievement of objectives to the senior manager (if you have one) and hold that person accountable for performance.
- Evaluate progress regularly.
- Re-evaluate goals and strategies periodically and adapt them when necessary to ensure that they remain relevant in a changing environment. Three years is now considered to be a realistic planning horizon for long-term business or strategic plans. This does not mean that longer-term 'visioning' or forecasting should be abandoned, just that the operating environment may be subject to rapid change that is often less predictable beyond these time horizons.

3.1.3   Inputs, activities, outputs and outcomes

There is often confusion about these terms. Simply put:

- *Inputs* are the resources (money, facilities, equipment, personnel, technology) used by an organization, program or project to achieve its objectives.
- *Activities* are the work and processes necessary to achieve the objectives, its outputs and outcomes.
- *Outputs* are the direct products that result from activities.
- *Outcomes* are the benefits flowing from activities and outputs to the stakeholders or recipients of the program.

Planning and evaluation involves identifying 'what outputs (*products*) create what outcomes (*benefits*) for whom (e.g., *client, member, community*) at what cost (*inputs*)'. For a more detailed discussion of these and other related terms and a logic model for planning and evaluation, see Parts 7.1: A logical framework for assessing results and 8.11: Evaluating performance. Refer also to Part 3.5: Performance monitoring and accountability.

3.2   FINANCIAL STEWARDSHIP — KEEPING TRACK OF THE MONEY AND ASSETS

> **Quick Tip**
>
> Learning to read financial statements and scrutinizing them thoroughly will give you a clear understanding of your organization's current fiscal realities, past trends and future prospects. (See Part 8.10: Template for financial monitoring).

The board is ultimately responsible for all aspects of an organization's performance. Financial stewardship merits particular attention because individual board members can incur personal financial liabilities for failure to exercise due diligence in this area. (See Parts 1.3: Duties and 1.4: Liabilities)

3.2.1   Securing resources – whose job is it anyway?

The board is directly responsible for *securing* adequate revenues for the safe, effective operation of the organization **or** for *ensuring* that such revenues are obtained. '*Safe*' means that revenues are sufficient to ensure that business can be reasonably conducted without placing volunteers, staff or consumers at undue risk. '*Effective*' means that revenues are sufficient to justify reasonable expectations that the organization's purpose can be fulfilled. There is a special onus on boards to prevail upon funders to support core (fixed) administrative costs that are essential to the survival and effectiveness of nonprofits, and for funders to recognize these costs. These include the costs of governing and managing the organization.

There is often confusion about whether revenue generation is a board or management (i.e., staff) function. The responsibility for securing revenues falls directly on board members in fledgling organizations and in organizations with operational boards (e.g., service clubs) or with a specific fundraising mandate (e.g., foundations). Boards with greater staff support may delegate some or all revenue generation authority to staff, but they cannot delegate the oversight responsibility of making sure that essential revenues are secured. As with other matters, the CEO and board must work in full partnership to ensure that the necessary revenues are secured.

There may be less need for direct board involvement in revenue generation in organizations that have fairly stable and predictable sources of revenue, such as those that depend on government sources. However, board vigilance is required to maintain organizational credibility, monitor trends, anticipate problems and manage risks. Boards should reserve the authority to approve all new funding initiatives (e.g., project grants, new funding streams and fundraising projects). It should also be up to the board to decide whether the organization will charge fees for service and how much it will charge.

Case Illustration: Importance of board oversight of finances and the funding environment

The Windsor Group Therapy Project was a nonprofit, publicly funded children's mental health organization, with a volunteer board of directors, providing services to vulnerable children. It was incorporated in 1956 but was dissolved in early 2000 after funding was withdrawn. A case study explored key issues of governance that led to or could have prevented the closing of this apparently effective and otherwise successful agency.

The study discovered that, overall, directors thought that they understood the programs of the agency and believed that they had been responsible in their discharge of legal and financial duties, and in their adherence to the requirements of the agency's funding sources. However, some were concerned about low board attendance and frequent turnover, over-reliance on the executive director for information and direction, and a less than optimal rapport with the funding partners in the decade immediately preceding the dissolution.

Quick Tip

The board is ultimately responsible for ensuring the continued funding of the organization. Consequently, it is important for the board to have a direct line of communication and relationship with funders and to understand funder priorities and other environmental factors that may affect its future funding.

Prospective candidates for the boards of service clubs, religious institutions, arts, cultural, recreational, sports organizations and community associations may suspect that they will be required to participate in fundraising. Nevertheless, these expectations should be clearly and explicitly stated when candidates are recruited. Indeed, members of any type of board may be expected to participate directly in fundraising during times of financial crisis or for exceptional capital and equipment projects. This, too, should be made clear at the time of recruitment. Most people join boards because they want to 'do good works' and to contribute to a cause to which they are committed, not because they want to raise money, a task with which they may be uncomfortable.

> **Quick Tip**
>
> When encouraging an entrepreneurial approach to the business and financing of your nonprofit, carefully assess financial risks and develop contingency plans for things that might go wrong.

Larger organizations that have an ongoing need for extra fundraising to supplement more stable revenue sources or support capital requirements may want to consider establishing a special fundraising committee or an arm's-length foundation with its own board. (See Appendix A.8.) Before a board takes this step, however, it should conduct a survey, preferably professional, to gauge community receptivity to any fundraising overtures. It should also bear in mind that major fundraising initiatives usually require substantial financial and staff support that could draw resources from the organization's primary mission. On the other hand, fundraising can raise the profile and credibility of an organization by attracting new community leaders and support.[45] See Part 3.5 for limitations on use of charitable revenues.

> **Quick Tip**
>
> An inventory of physical assets can be most easily developed and maintained at the time of purchase…it's always more difficult to play catch-up when substantial equipment has been accumulated without being recorded in an inventory file.

3.2.2   Assets

Assets may be physical (buildings and equipment), cash reserves or, less tangibly, community reputation. The board is responsible for ensuring that these are properly and prudently managed and safeguarded.

Many organizations have found themselves in serious financial difficulty after depleting cash reserves to subsidize ongoing operating costs without developing any plan to replenish those reserves. Too often boards have paid insufficient attention to the use of reserves and have placed too much trust in the CEO's budget and reporting practices.

> **Case Illustration – Assets and un-funded liabilities**
>
> The Canadian Council on Social Development (CCSD) is a prestigious national research, social policy and education association founded in 1920. The early 1990s was a critical transitional phase for the organization. A long-serving CEO resigned in 1990, leaving no business plan to support the mission. Accounting was weak; a funding crisis was looming; a 'permanent' unionized staff complement, unsustainable with decreasing revenues, created un-funded contingent liabilities; substantial debt had accumulated; membership records were poor; the board was able to meet only twice a year, placing excessive onus on the executive committee and CEO; and the board was operating with a 'lifeboat' mentality in which the major focus was financial survival.

In the words of one former board chair, "In a crisis of this sort, governance models go out the window. Policy issues were dwarfed in comparative importance to the very real prospect of financial insolvency." There was real resistance to reducing the board size as well as considerable agonizing over the need for the eventual staff layoffs. CCSD had to sell a large headquarters building that it owned in order to stave off creditors and allow it to restructure and become a leaner, more efficient and more entrepreneurial operation. The cost of this experience was high but the organization showed enormous resiliency and is now on stable footing.

3.2.3 Un-funded liabilities

Un-funded or contingent liabilities carry with them the possibility of bankruptcy, which could force dissolution of an organization. Un-funded liabilities may occur when contractual obligations to staff or suppliers exceed the organization's revenue capacity. For example, organizations that rely on project funding or other non-continuous funding could find themselves with un-funded liabilities if they commit to permanent employment of staff without any permanent source of revenue to pay those staff. Organizations can also face un-funded liabilities if they have not set aside enough reserve or contingency funds to deal with sick leave or severance pay. Un-funded liability becomes a particular concern for boards that must dissolve their organizations because directors may become liable for some costs related to unpaid salaries and benefits.

Quick Tips

Make long-term commitments only if you have a 'reasonable' expectation that you will have the revenue to cover them. Calculate the cost of contingent liabilities and set aside sufficient reserve funds to offset them. Maintain board control of reserve funds and monitor expenditure trends closely.

Require specific board authorization to draw down reserve funds, whether for capital or operating purposes.

Case Illustration – Assets and un-funded liabilities

The Canadian Institute for Child Health (CICH) was established with an endowment in 1977. By 1987, it had accumulated a reserve of some $500,000. But by the late 1980s it had depleted all but $100,000 of its reserve in order to support its annual operations. Discontinuity in executive leadership during the late '80s, combined with a board that was composed primarily of professionals who were more concerned with the 'work' of the Institute than with governance and financial oversight, contributed to this situation. Termination of core funding from Health Canada in 1994 exacerbated the financial crisis.

continued overleaf

continued from previous page

There was a period of relative stability in the mid to late 1990s, thanks to a corporate sponsorship program (Council of Patrons) and more consistent staff leadership. But lessons from past mistakes in financial stewardship had not been carried forward. In 2003 the CICH board made a difficult decision to layoff 90% of its workforce, despite some incomplete projects, and faced the prospect of winding down the corporation.

The good news was that board members rallied and did what was necessary to save the organization to which they had substantial professional and personal attachment. They concluded that the problem that had precipitated the most recent crisis was use of a cash rather than accrual accounting method. This was exacerbated by the unanticipated departure of a long-serving executive director, which resulted in a loss of corporate memory.

Following short tenures by two part-time, interim CEOs, a board member took on the senior management functions on a volunteer basis to tide the organization over until new project revenues could be secured. Other board members and volunteers took over organization of CICH's major fundraising gala. The board established a local 'management committee' to provide support and direction to the organization. It also undertook development of a new business model to diversify revenues; shifted its primary publication, "The Health of Canada's Children," from a print to a less expensive Web-based publication and entered a new research partnership with the University of Ottawa.

This example illustrates the importance of a board's resiliency in adapting its governance approach (from a traditional to a management board) to respond to changing circumstances and crises. It also demonstrates the importance of board members' commitment to the organization's cause.

3.2.4   The annual operating budget

The annual operating budget (revenues and expenditures) and operational plan approved by the board form the board's basis for monitoring current year performance. These should always be reviewed in the context of past history and future projections. The board should receive monthly, or at least quarterly, reports on year-to-date actual revenues and expenditures with future in-year projections to ensure that the organization is on-track with the budget plan and to anticipate potential deficit problems or surplus windfalls. It is important for the board to maintain sufficient independence from management to satisfy itself that reports are reliable and to ensure financial integrity. (See Section 8.10: Template for financial monitoring.)

Boards are responsible for ensuring that accounting practices conform to 'Generally Accepted Accounting Principles (GAAP)', that proper audits are conducted and that problems identified in the auditor's 'management letters' are corrected or that there is a good and reasonable argument for disagreeing with and not acting on specific recommendations. In general, it is the board's job to decide whether the advice in a management letter ought to be implemented; however, it ignores this advice at its own peril.

But, separation of accounting responsibilities and signing authorities, an important GAAP principle, may simply be impractical in small organizations. In such instances it is important to have a board member as one of two required signing authorities.

3.2.5 Expense accounts and loans

Many a board or CEO has been compromised by failure to exercise proper oversight of expense claims. The board chair or treasurer should be charged with the responsibility to approve expense claims from the CEO and board members and to ensure that these fall within established limits (and that established limits are reasonable and justifiable). At the very least, either the board chair or the treasurer should review expense claims quarterly. Under no circumstances should nonprofit or public sector organizations extend personal loans to board members or staff.

Case Illustrations: Betrayed trust/failed oversight

In 1992, the United Way of America investigated allegations of mismanagement against its long-time president, William Aramony. "He was accused of using charitable donations to finance a lavish lifestyle, including support of an expensive condominium, use of a limousine, and trips on the Concorde. Other allegations included his involvement in satellite corporations, spun off from the main UWA operation. His salary of $463,000, including fringe benefits, also fueled the fires of public outrage" and compromised the credibility of the organization.[46]

In a substantially more obscene abuse of power, Bernie Eberts, chair and CEO of embattled WorldCom, was charged in 2003 with fraud for misappropriating (borrowing) millions of dollars to purchase private property and support a lavish lifestyle. Other glaring examples include the CEOs of Enron, Tyco and others.

3.3   HUMAN RESOURCES STEWARDSHIP — CARING FOR THE PEOPLE RESOURCES

A high proportion of the resources of most nonprofit and public sector organizations go to human resources, primarily to staff salaries and benefits. Salaries and benefits typically account for between 60 percent and 95 percent of available operating revenues, depending on the size of the organization and its capital equipment requirements.

A Gallup Organization survey of over one million employees and 80,000 managers in 400 companies provides remarkable insight into the difference well-managed human resources can make in helping organizations realize excellence and good results. Choosing the right people to do the right work supported by the right managers with sufficient authority is characteristic of excellent organizations. Indeed, the Gallup research discovered that the biggest difference between excellent corporations that achieve great results and other organizations is the quality of managers they have working for them.[47]

The findings suggest that managers make the difference, not company policy and procedures, policy manuals, or organizational structures. Furthermore, managers who are closest to front-line action have the biggest impact on quality, productivity and results.

The Gallup findings also suggest that great managers are distinguished by their leadership qualities, rather than by their administrative proficiency, professional competence or internal seniority. These leadership qualities include:

- a commitment to ethical behavior, personal excellence and achievement;
- goal orientation with 'big picture' conceptual strength; and
- strong interpersonal skills, combined with a capacity to stimulate, motivate, persuade, invest in the development of others and derive satisfaction from team success.

Each role in an organization, no matter how modest, requires talent, valuation and recognition. Great managers are catalysts that turn talent into performance. They are students of excellence, not of failure. Talent, unlike specific task skills, cannot be taught; it is innate.[48] As the saying goes, 'You cannot make a silk purse out of a sow's ear'.

The right fit between talent, task and motivation is important to job satisfaction at every level within an organization. This is true for both staff and volunteers (including those who serve on the board). Finding the right fit is key to staff and volunteer recruitment and selection. If circumstances change so that particular staff or volunteers no longer seem to have a good talent, task or motivation fit with the organization, they should be encouraged, in a fair and respectful manner, to seek opportunities elsewhere. This is especially true for the most senior management positions within the organization.

Those organizations that wish to promote excellence will be sensitive to the professional and personal needs of staff, volunteers and those they serve. They will be supportive of their efforts to make a positive contribution to the achievement of the organization's objectives and to their own personal and professional development.

> **Quick Tip**
>
> Staff and volunteers are the engines that power nonprofits. Recognize volunteer contributions with public acknowledgement. Reward superior staff performance with compensation, training and promotion based on merit as well as peer and public recognition.

3.3.1 Selecting a competent CEO – the board's most important responsibility

The CEO is the board's most important partner in developing and executing its policies and achieving its goals. Selecting, supporting and regularly evaluating the performance of the CEO is the board's most important responsibility. In a stable organization with a well functioning board, CEO selection is likely to be an infrequent task. But turnover is inevitable. All organizations will have to replace a CEO eventually. Boards often view this as a problem rather than as an opportunity to review and revitalize the organization's direction.[49] Before the board recruits a CEO, it is critical for all board members to be clear on the goals of the organization and the characteristics essential in a CEO who can best help the organization to achieve those goals.

> **Quick Tips**
>
> Board members may not have the expertise necessary to conduct a thorough search and screening of potential candidates. If your organization can afford it, hire an executive search firm. Some search firms offer discounted rates or limited pro bono services to smaller nonprofits.
>
> Whether or not you use a search firm, make sure that you do your own reference checks and ask probing questions. Always obtain transcripts to verify academic credentials.

A CEO must have management competence, the board's confidence and trust, and a personal leadership style that fits with that of the board. The board should make its expectations of the CEO clear during the selection process and throughout the board/CEO partnership. This is essential to building trust and providing ongoing guidance and evaluation of the CEO's performance.

Similarly, the CEO's expectations of the board are a key element of a constructive working partnership grounded in mutual trust and respect. The annual performance expectations of the CEO should be established through negotiation between the board and CEO in the context of the board's long-term plan for the organization. This should be a practical plan that is developed in full consultation with the CEO.

Once the board has selected the CEO, it is responsible for providing support, guidance, advice and regular feedback about performance based on objective criteria. The CEO may seek advice from board committees, individual board members and the chair. However, only the full board can provide formal direction. "The litmus test of the chief executive's leadership is not the ability to solve problems alone, but the capacity to articulate key questions and guide a collaborative effort to formulate answers."[50]

If serious conflicts develop in the board/CEO relationship or if the board loses confidence in the CEO, the board should move quickly to resolve the conflict or terminate the relationship. (See Part 6.2.10.)

3.3.2   Staff and volunteer resources

Operational, management and collective boards inevitably have a high degree of direct involvement in staff matters. However, organizations that have an executive director must delegate to that person the responsibility **and** authority for day-to-day management of staff, within the parameters of its human resources policies. This delegation does not, however, absolve the board of responsibility for ensuring sound human resources practices.

Boards must ensure that there are clear job descriptions for staff and volunteers (including board members); establish human resources policies that comply with relevant legislation and common law requirements (e.g., labor and employment standards, administrative and common law requirements for due process and fair employment practices, human rights, workplace harassment, privacy, etc.); and monitor compliance with these. The board should also monitor compliance with criteria for employment, and trends related to such human resources matters as attendance, sick leave, workers compensation claims, grievances and critical incidents (e.g., assaults on, or complaints against, staff or volunteers).

> **Quick Tip**
>
> Your organization's human resources policies for both staff and volunteers should reflect the organization's core values.

3.3.3   Dealing with staff, staff associations and unions

While members of management and collective boards may be directly involved with staff and/or clients, boards of larger organizations will not normally have such direct dealings except through committee work or formal complaints or representations to the board. However, through the budgeting process, the board is responsible for establishing the guidelines within which management negotiates staff compensation (salaries, benefits and working conditions) and for ensuring that management acts within these guidelines.

It is particularly important to understand that the board is the legal employer of staff, even though staff report to the CEO. Many organizations have staff associations or unions that negotiate salaries, benefits and working conditions on behalf of staff groups. Management of these negotiations should be delegated to the CEO, who may conduct them directly, through staff, or, where affordable, through labor relations professionals. An exception to this rule is boards that are under a statutory obligation to directly participate in or manage collective bargaining (e.g., some police and school boards). Even in these instances, however, professional labor negotiators should be engaged.

Disagreements or conflicts are common during collective bargaining, and can become protracted or public. Board members should resist the temptation to get involved in these conflicts. Their interference can be costly in financial terms and can undermine management's authority, not just in the negotiations but in all other matters. Such interference often leads to the loss of a competent CEO by career choice or through a constructive dismissal process.

> **Quick Tip**
>
> Don't undermine your CEO by interfering in staff/management relations. This is especially important during a period of an open contract with a unionized work force.

The board is also responsible for ensuring that management has established fair processes for dealing with staff/union grievances and complaints; for requesting and reviewing reports on the frequency and disposition of such incidents; and for taking this information into consideration when developing or modifying board polices. But most boards should not become directly involved in these matters. Operational, management and collective boards are, by their nature, an exception to this general 'hands-off' advice.

3.3.4 Succession planning

Succession planning, both for the board and senior management, is an important board task. When done correctly, it helps improve and strengthen the performance of the board and of management. A strong nominations process (See Section 6.1: Board development) will increase your chances of getting board members with the right talents and motivations who are able to undertake the tasks that need to be done. Similarly, following the principles presented in the introduction to this section (3.3: Human resources stewardship) will increase the likelihood of sound succession planning for senior management. Boards should also

> **Quick Tip**
>
> If a board member wishes to compete for any staff position, that board member should first resign from the board. If the board member is not successful in winning the staff position, he or she should not return to the board during the tenure of the CEO who made that staffing decision. The same should be required of a board member who steps into the CEO position for an interim period.

ensure that the CEO has a succession planning process in place for other staff. This should include job descriptions (task, talent and qualifications requirements), career assessments, job rotation and training.

Case Illustrations: Conflicts arising from CEO transitions

The chair of an Association for Community Living twice took leave from the board to step into its CEO position on an interim basis. Each time a new CEO was hired, the chair-interim CEO resumed the position of board chair.

A board member of a community health association competed unsuccessfully for its CEO spot but remained on the board.

In both instances, this created unnecessary undercurrents of second-guessing and conflict.

3.4   PERFORMANCE MONITORING AND ACCOUNTABILITY

Another important responsibility of any board of directors is to monitor the performance of the organization, and to measure and account for its results. An organization's performance can be assessed against its own past performance, against the performance of other organizations in the same business or against established standards or benchmarks for a service. Accreditation programs or more specific 'industry' standards may establish preferred ratios for inputs (e.g., staff/client or time/task), outputs (e.g., services delivered, operations completed) or outcomes (e.g., rehabilitation rates, educational achievement). (See Part 8.11: Evaluating performance, for further discussion of these concepts.)

There are five components to performance monitoring and accountability. They are:

  i. development and/or custodianship (safeguarding) of the organization's purpose, mandate and identity;
  ii. ensuring that the organization's mission remains respectful of its historical legacy and responsive to changes in the social, economic and fiscal environment in which the organization operates;
  iii. trusteeship of financial resources to ensure that funds are expended for the purposes intended;
  iv. stewardship of services to ensure that intended beneficiaries receive their entitlements; and
  v. responsibility and reporting to the 'primary owners', i.e., the members who elect the board or funders who appoint it (shareholders in the 'for-profit' sector) as well as to other stakeholders and the general public.

Accountability is the requirement to explain and accept responsibility for carrying out an assigned mandate in light of expectations agreed upon with the organization's owners (members or 'stake/shareholders') and funders or investors. This means:

- **Regular communication** with, and proper accounting to, financial investors (funders or donors) and other key stakeholders. Communication is at the heart of accountability. The most common and effective methods of communication are newsletters (paper and electronic), annual meetings and reports, Web postings, focus groups, surveys and media communications.
- **Regular monitoring** of organizational performance. This is is essential to accountability.
- **Evaluation**. This must be built upon reliable information that is the 'best available' within the limits of current resources. Systems must be designed to gather information that, in so far as possible, allows fair and impartial assessment of the organization's achievements in meeting pre-established objectives, using agreed-upon criteria or indicators.
- **Development of a fair, formal complaints process.** This is a benchmark of proper accountability to the beneficiaries of an organization's activities, i.e., its individual or organizational members, donors, or the recipients (clients/ consumers) of its goods or services.

Quick Tip

A fair complaints process focuses on whether established rules/policies were followed, whether those involved received fair treatment and what changes in rules might be advised. It should provide for recommendations to the board with respect to rules or policies and to management with respect to implementation of the rules. It should avoid interference in staff decisions unless there has been willful negligence, serious error or intentional subversion of the rules, and management has refused to act. In such cases, there are obviously more serious issues to be resolved between the board and CEO.

Although outcomes evaluation can lead to a high level of accountability, it can be both tricky and costly. Whereas in business enterprises, bottom-line profit/loss and share value are readily measured, in nonprofits, 'outcomes' are often difficult to define and assess. It may be difficult, if not impossible, to link project activities to subsequent consequences, i.e., to establish a cause-and-effect relationship between the activities, the outputs and the desired outcomes. Therefore, keeping evaluation simple is strongly advised.

Identifying and monitoring 'inputs' and 'outputs' and trends related to these is less difficult, but it still requires a systematic approach to information gathering, a clear focus and substantial resources. Securing adequate resources (including knowledge) to support effective governance

Quick Tip

You can add rigor to your planning and performance evaluation by using a systematic, logical framework, but don't become obsessive in its application. (See Part 7.1)

and to measure organizational performance is a continuing challenge for boards and funders. A basic framework for planning and evaluation is contained in Section 7.1: A logical framework for planning and assessing results, and elaborated in 8.11: Evaluating performance.

3.4.1   What to monitor

Because monitoring and evaluation can be expensive and time-consuming, it's important to focus on aspects of your operations that are reasonable measures of performance and that can be realistically gauged. Build performance-monitoring systems around the following principles and practices:

- Keep track of the money. This is fundamental to fulfilling fiduciary and stewardship obligations. Monitor year-to-year and monthly or quarterly results and projections on key revenue and expenditure lines and watch the trends. Calculate costs per unit of input, per activity and per output. Compare present performance to past performance. Compare your organization to similar organizations.
- Identify the areas (services or products) in which you expect results. Define specific objectives within each area and identify the indicators that will let you know whether you have achieved the desired results or whether progress is being made.
- Measure and assess trends in the key services or activities provided by your organization, e.g., activity levels, client volume, reports produced, consultations, fundraising programs, events organized, etc.
- Undertake accreditation reviews if resources permit. Performance benchmarks within sectors are often established through accreditation programs, by regulatory authority or by professional practice standards. In most cases, these are either process or output standards. The board and CEO can adopt or adapt the standards that are most relevant to their operations, regardless of whether a full accreditation survey is undertaken.

Quick Tip

The process standards that make up most accreditation programs assume that if certain generally accepted practices have been followed, then certain positive 'outcomes' may be presumed. Examples of 'output' benchmarks are industry averages for measures such as 'crime clearance' and 'conviction' rates for police services, 'investigations completed' (within specified time periods) for child protection agencies, 'specific surgical procedures' in hospitals, 'client visits or sessions' in social services and community health agencies, and 'events held' for community arts, recreation and sporting groups. Such measures can be used to compare your organization's current year performance against that of previous years or against that of organizations with a similar mandate. These measures may also be used as proxy measures of productivity. When paired with unit cost information, they become a measure of efficiency. (See Parts 3.1.2, 3.1.3, 7.1 and 8.11 for more detailed guidance on this topic.)

- Evaluate compliance with policies established by the board. These could include limits on spending authority for capital acquisitions, expense claims, guidelines for staff compensation, service standards and human resources policies, etc.
- Keep track of human resources. People power is the engine that drives any organization. Tracking human resources (staff and volunteers) is as important as tracking the money. Among the key indicators of performance in this area are staff numbers, turnover or retention rates, education levels, job classifications, compensation, attendance, training costs, severance costs, worker's compensation claims, and complaints or grievances. Remember also that performance commendations are an important component of volunteer and employee motivation and another useful indicator of human resources performance.
- Review any information that may have been gathered from periodic surveys of employees and volunteers. This can help you identify trends and monitor overall performance. Similarly, surveys and trend analysis of client satisfaction and consumer/client complaints may also be a useful planning adjunct.
- Monitor media reports to gauge public perceptions of your organization.
- Monitor board performance (see section 6.2.3).

Quick Tip

Most organizations have limited resources. Identify key indicators of success in achieving your objectives. Measure what matters most to the overall success of the organization.

3.5   COMMUNITY REPRESENTATION, EDUCATION AND ADVOCACY

Board members are responsible for:

- promoting the organization in the community;
- representing member, stakeholder and community interests;
- ensuring fair stakeholder representation (including ethnic and cultural diversity) through the nominations process; and
- facilitating stakeholder input to planning.

In short, board members are 'good will' ambassadors and advocates for their organization and are responsible for representing community interests to the organization. Education, an important component of advocacy, serves primarily to inform the community about your organization and to improve the community's understanding of the organization. Advocacy, which is more assertive and usually non-partisan, attempts to influence others or persuade them to adopt a particular point of view or support a particular cause or initiative. Education and advocacy are essential to establishing the good reputation of the organization, securing resources and promoting the organization's objectives.

The essential tools and tactics for effective education and advocacy are:

Essential Tools	Essential Tactics
• Committed leadership • Clear objectives • Solid research • Grassroots support • Well-organized education/lobby efforts • Smart (internal and external) communications strategy	• Know where power resides • Appeal to self-interest - seek commitments • Mount intensive education/advocacy campaigns • Generate public awareness • Nurture political responsiveness • Build alliances; seek common ground • Focus on what's essential or what may be a good first step (consider reasonable comprises in exchange for achievable results) • Understand opponents • Push the 'right buttons' • Work with allies in the ranks of elected officials, their staff and bureaucrats • Nurture non-traditional partners

There are some restrictions on advocacy by registered charities. For example, Canadian charities are required to expend "substantially all" of their funds (generally interpreted as 90%) on the primary objects of their incorporation. This means they are generally limited to spending no more than 10% of their resources on non-partisan political activities. Certain exceptions may be made to this limit for smaller charities or for 'short-term, one-of-a-kind expenditures'. The Canada Revenue Agency has stated that:

"They [registered charities] may choose to advance their charitable purposes by taking part in non-partisan political activities if they are connected and subordinate to those charitable purposes. This means that a charity may make the public aware of its position on an issue provided that public awareness campaigns do not become the charity's primary activity.

"They are prohibited from using their resources for [a] partisan political activity; one that involves direct or indirect support of, or opposition to, any political party or candidate for public office...or seek[s] to retain, oppose, or change the law, policy, or decision of any level of government in Canada or a foreign country."[51]

> **Quick Tips**
>
> ◆ Be clear about your mission and the messages that you want to communicate.
> ◆ Identify the primary audience(s) to which your message(s) will be directed.
> ◆ Communicate regularly with members, funders and other key stakeholders.
> ◆ Take credit for achievements.
> ◆ Accept responsibility for mistakes (but coordinate these messages with legal counsel and insurers).
> ◆ Equip your media spokespersons and good will ambassadors (board members, volunteers and staff) with information, support and training.
> ◆ Develop a contingency plan to respond to potential crises.

3.5.1 Dealing with the media

Many organizations have found themselves in difficulty when several board or staff members deliver conflicting messages. The media are quick to seize upon and magnify internal or external conflict. It is recommended that the board designate the board chair (or some other board member skilled in media communications) as the chief public spokesperson for the organization with respect to board policies and overarching matters that affect the organization as a whole and its standing in the community. The CEO should be the public spokesperson on operational matters or should delegate this responsibility to the appropriate staff. When there is overlap between the two, messages should be clear and carefully coordinated. A board that has not established clear policies on media relations and prepared its spokesperson may be ill equipped to respond in a credible manner.

> **Quick Tips**
>
> - Get to know the differences between the news, editorial and features departments of the local paper.
> - Cultivate positive relationships with journalists.
> - Avoid fights with people who, in the words of former baseball coach Tommy Lasorta, 'buy ink by the barrel'.
> - Remember that journalists like to focus on complaints, crises, catastrophes, conflicts, controversies, competition, contradictions and, sometimes compassion...and prefer to deal with them in 15-second sound bites or quotes, too often out-of-context. Stay on message!
> - Use meetings with the editorial board, op-ed pieces and letters to the editor to your advantage.
> - Opt for live, rather than taped, interviews if you have a choice.
> - Enlist external champions to help advocate your cause.

3.6   RISK MANAGEMENT

Risk is *the possibility that adverse consequences may flow from a decision, an action or a failure to act.* The potential for risk is present whenever a decision is made to pursue (or not pursue) new opportunities or confront new challenges. All organizations face the potential for risks to financial stability; un-funded liabilities; criminal or civil litigation related to staff or board malfeasance, injury to staff, volunteers or clients; losses on fundraising or entrepreneurial ventures; and loss of community credibility. A favorable community reputation can be easily squandered but is painstakingly recovered.

> **Case Illustrations: Squandered reputations and financial losses**
>
> Several years ago, ticket sales for a lottery organized by the Canadian Olympic Association fell short of projections. This forced the governing body for Canada's Olympic movement to dip into an endowment fund to cover losses.
>
> More recently, the Canadian Diabetes Association ran a deficit after losing $7.1 million in a bungled lottery. The fiasco – the result of poor ticket sales – prompted top volunteers in Toronto to resign. It also resulted in the resignation of the association's executive director.[52]

Risk management is forward-looking. It is about anticipating and controlling, to the extent possible, foreseeable future adversities.[53] The first defense against risk is to ensure sound governance, management, and professional practices and standards. The following approach will aid that defense.

- Ensure that the organization has adequate resources to conduct its affairs safely and without undue risk to staff, clients and volunteers.
- Ensure that Generally Accepted Accounting Principles (GAAP) are used in keeping the organization's financial records.
- Require board approval (and record its rationale) for any financial or business practice that a reasonably prudent person might consider unorthodox or that might create financial liability beyond the normal conduct of business.
- Ensure that an independent financial audit is conducted annually and either redress any problems identified in the auditor's 'management letter' or establish a sound rationale for discounting that advice.
- Develop a risk assessment and management program that identifies actual or potential risks, protects against them, and regularly monitors and reports on risks and steps taken to mitigate them.
- Develop contingency plans for foreseeable risks.
- Submit to the scrutiny of a relevant accreditation body and fix what it identifies as in need of repair. Strive for even better results in areas identified as strengths.
- Develop a quality management system in conformance with business process standards set by the ISO (International Organization for Standardization) to either complement or provide an alternative to other accreditation processes. Registering as an ISO-approved organization assures that your organization has complied with ISO standards as judged by an independent audit. Note, however, that unlike certain accreditation programs, the ISO process does not attempt to assess quality of services, that it is resource- and time-intensive and may, therefore, be beyond the reach of many nonprofits.
- Review bylaws and governance policies regularly to ensure that they conform to periodically changing provisions of incorporation legislation and other changing circumstances.
- Regularly monitor actual practices to ensure compliance with bylaws and governance policies.
- Follow the advice offered elsewhere in this handbook to enhance protection against risks, particularly Part 1.3: Duties of individual directors.
- Refer to Parts 1.4: Liabilities and 3.7: Critical events for additional circumstances that may give rise to risk.

A directors indemnification clause in the bylaws, as well as 'general', 'errors and omissions' and 'directors and officers' liability insurance, provide an important safety net. However, these should be the last, not the only, lines of defense.

Case Illustrations: Inconsistencies between bylaws, policies and practices

My case study research revealed that bylaw provisions and policies were sometimes inconsistent with each other or with practice, or were internally inconsistent or at odds with corporations legislation. For example:

The bylaws of three national organizations identified the board chair as the chief executive officer of the organization and made no provision for appointment of an executive director even though, in practice, each had appointed a person to such a position under the general board authority to appoint staff. In two cases this created real confusion about the roles of the chair and the executive director.

In other organizations, provisions for nominating committees were not followed, committees were established even though there was no specific bylaw authority that allowed for their establishment and, contrary to the Corporations Act, proxy voting at board meetings was permitted and quorum for board meetings was set at 40%.

In one instance, the bylaws empowered the CEO to define the responsibilities of board officers. This created a risk that the lines of accountability would be reversed.

Quick Tips

Compliance with established policies will mitigate risk. There is less risk associated with high compliance with fewer policies than there is with lax compliance with a large number of policies.

Important documents and files should be stored safely and securely. Electronic files should be backed up regularly and the back-ups stored off-site.

You should prepare for any risk that is reasonably foreseeable. Develop contingency plans for foreseeable threats such as staff work stoppages or potential public controversies. Make sure these plans include a media and stakeholder communications strategy.

3.7   MANAGEMENT OF CRITICAL EVENTS AND TRANSITIONAL PHASES

There are certain critical events and transitional phases that are typical to all organizations. Transitional phases are often referred to as the 'life cycle' of an organization. Although some of these events or phases are clearly associated with the organizational or founding period of an organization, there is little evidence to support the notion that they are linked to the age of an organization or that one follows the other in a sequential, linear path. There is, however, considerable support for the view that critical phases occur at key transitional points in an organization's evolution. Examples of critical events and transitional phases are:

- legal incorporation;
- recruitment of first staff;
- significant milestones in the growth of staff and/or budget;
- significant downsizing in staff and/or budget;
- substantive change in mandate, either internally initiated or externally imposed;
- merger with another organization or funder-imposed discussions about merger or service realignment;
- attempts to make significant shifts in organizational culture;
- loss of key board members or the CEO;
- turnover of significant numbers of board members;
- major external conflict (with collateral agencies, funders, media, public);
- major internal conflict (e.g., within the board or staff group, between board members and management or between staff and management, such as conflicts in collective bargaining or in the workplace);
- major public/media controversy (e.g., death or injury to client or staff; criminal charges or civil litigation against the organization, staff or volunteers; or public exposure of internal conflicts);
- significant changes in the financial, political or policy environment; and
- significant dissatisfaction in client or other key stakeholder groups.

Transitional phases and critical events occur infrequently in the life of a healthy organization. When they do, the role of the board is to provide a 'safety-net' for the organization by backing-up the CEO, who may need a little extra support to manage the issue or threat in question. Some consider this to be analogous to the role of firefighters, who suffer through the tedium of a lot of 'down-time' but who must train so that they are well prepared to respond to an emergency fire call.

Case Illustration: Board/CEO partnership in managing a crisis

The Children's Aid Society of Ottawa Carleton found itself under intense public and media attack in the mid-90s when it was discovered that infants had been mistakenly switched during adoptions decades earlier. The 'twins' case was profiled in a national and international media storm. Members of the board rallied to the agency's support, met with the editorial board of the local newspaper and helped to develop a legal and media response strategy, including media interviews with the board chair. This took some of the heat off the agency. It also reinforced the role of the board in ensuring current standards of good practice and accountability on behalf of the public, and assisting in crisis management. This approach also reaffirmed the responsibility of the CEO for addressing current operational matters. The full board partnership with the CEO in coordinating messages was critical to minimizing damage to the agency's reputation. *Note: Based on the author's personal experience.*

See also Case Illustrations in Parts 3.2.2 (CCSD) and 3.2.3 (CICH).

Quick Tip

The emergence of any critical phase is likely to draw the governing board into the day-to-day operations of the organization to at least some degree. This is a critical time for the board and the organization. Too much involvement is likely to divert the board from its governance function; too little may leave the organization adrift. The normal division of responsibilities between the board and management should be restored as quickly as possible. The board should take care to intervene only with an eye to the future. Remember that actions taken today may restrict or broaden tomorrow's options, and strengthen or weaken relationships.

Part Four – Nonprofit Structures

4.1 The legal framework

The following outline applies generally to the legal status of nonprofits, but may vary somewhat according to jurisdiction. Consult legal counsel for specific information on incorporation and on tax exempt and charitable status in your jurisdiction.

Incorporated nonprofit. Incorporation of a nonprofit organization establishes it as a legal entity. It may hold assets, borrow money, incur legal liability and limit the personal liability of its directors. Incorporated nonprofits in Canada are exempt from income tax. Incorporated nonprofits in the United States must make a separate application for tax-exempt status after a state approves its incorporation.

Nonprofit and public sector organizations may be incorporated or established under one or more of the following:

- federal or provincial/state corporations legislation;
- nonprofit corporations (societies) acts;
- federal or provincial/state cooperatives legislation; and
- 'Special Purposes' legislation such as that establishing hospitals, universities, school boards, federal, provincial/state agencies or (crown) corporations.

Registered charity. Subject to certain criteria, a nonprofit may also be registered as a charity to obtain authority to issue tax receipts for charitable donations, which permits donors to deduct all or a portion of contributions from personal or corporate income tax.

Unincorporated association. Many nonprofits operate without going through the legal incorporation process, which can be expensive and time-consuming and is often unnecessary if the organization does not have a large budget, does not want to issue tax receipts for donations or has no need to account for expenditure of public revenues.

"The most common classification system in the U. S. contains three categories: mutual benefit organizations (organizations which primarily serve the interests of their members); public benefit organizations (which includes charities that are not religious institutions); and religious organizations."[54]

4.2   WHO OWNS THE ORGANIZATION?

Ownership is a concept that is not generally applied to nonprofit organizations. However, it is important to sound accountability to understand who 'owns' the organization. Ownership can be traced by identifying the individuals or bodies that have the right to elect or appoint (and remove) members of the organization's board of directors and, in some instances, the board chair or other officers. Most commonly, it is members of nonprofit corporations that hold this right. In some instances the members of the board of directors are the sole members of the corporation.

The board of directors of the nonprofit is the legal entity that is accountable for the conduct of an organization's affairs. It carries the membership and broader 'public trust' vested in a nonprofit organization, even though staff may be delegated to carry out its work. To be accountable is to accept responsibility for and to explain the conduct of the business within the parameters of the purposes stated in the corporation's bylaws, its contractual obligations, applicable legislation and regulations, and approved policies.

Many boards carry on business as though ownership were vested in the board of directors rather than in the members. They focus their attention on the relationship between the board and CEO, which, although vital, is not the only relationship that is important for sound accountability. Accountability requirements flow from responsibilities to owners, other key stakeholders and the terms of contractual arrangements, and statutory and regulatory provisions.

Identifying the 'owners' of the organization is essential to establishing proper accountability mechanisms and open lines of communication. Incorporation documents identify who holds authority to elect or appoint the board. These are the owners of the organization. However, it is also important to provide an accounting to' non-owner' stakeholders to whom the organization may have either a fiduciary or moral obligation.

Most nonprofit and public sector boards are incorporated under federal, provincial/state (nonprofit) corporations or societies legislation. Some are incorporated under cooperatives legislation. Many (such as hospitals, universities, school boards, child welfare agencies, crown agencies) receive their mandate through designation under special purposes legislation such as hospitals, education or child welfare or crown corporations acts. Each method of incorporation and mandate designation has its own unique implications for ownership structure and accountability practices.

The following classification of nonprofit boards, according to the process used for selecting the board, may be helpful to boards that wish to clearly define their lines of accountability. (Appendix C contains a more detailed description of these.)

Selection Process	Ownership & Primary Accountability	Secondary Accountability
Founding (Organizing Board): consensus or self-selected	Founding board members	Funders, consumers, public, staff and volunteers
Self-Regenerating	Board members	As above
Funder Appointed	Funding authority	Consumers, public, staff, volunteers
Membership elected	Members	Funders, consumers, public, staff and volunteers
Publicly elected	Eligible voters or taxpayer electorate	As above
Mixed selection process (two or more of the above)	Multiple constituencies	As above

Founding and self-regenerating boards are legally accountable only to themselves. Boards that are appointed by a government, funding authority or other controlling body are legally accountable to that body. Members own organizations with an active, rather than a nominal, membership base. The boards of organizations with only a nominal or inactive membership have effective or practical ownership control, although the broader membership holds legal ownership. Boards that act as though they have no accountability to a broader member base or public constituency may find themselves in difficulty for failure to properly consider the interests of those constituents and account to them for their actions. Boards that are publicly elected are accountable to the electorate. Those that have taxation powers, such as school boards, are accountable to the taxpayer electorate. A mixture of two or more of these processes is used to select the boards of some nonprofits.

Collectives and chartered or affiliate organizational forms have somewhat unique ownership structures. Staff, and sometimes consumers and a general membership, may exercise effective (ownership) control over selection of the board of a collective. The members of a chartered organization or affiliate, own organizations that are created under the authority of an international, national or provincial chartering body but owe special accountability to the values and purposes of the chartering body, which has the authority to revoke the charter.

> **Quick Tip**
>
> Organizations with a geographically dispersed membership should take special care to ensure that members who live in locations that are remote from where the general meeting is held are given adequate opportunity, through proxies or other means, to participate in membership meetings.

Case Illustration: Owners given less weight than other stakeholders

A study of school board governance in Canada suggested that trustees give more weight to the opinions of teachers and students than to electors, who are the legal owners of school boards. They also give more weight to electors than they do to the education ministry that funds school boards and provides their mandate.

Quick Tip

He who pays the piper calls the tune. Give due consideration to the interests of financial investors/ supporters, e.g., granting or contracting authorities, donors and fee-paying clients. Don't bite the hands that feed you.

Lines of accountability are blurred when selection processes are 'mixed' (when two or more different processes are used to fill different director positions) or when different groups of stakeholders have unequal power. This often contributes to a climate of confusion and conflict surrounding the roles, allegiances and accountability of board members, especially when powerful stakeholders have differing positions on issues. This can lead to situations where individuals who have greater access to decision-makers or greater power to influence decisions, subvert or usurp the authority of legal owners.

Case Illustration: Mixed selection process causes dual allegiances

Boards of Regional Health Districts in Saskatchewan were selected through such a 'mixed process'. The provincial government, which was the primary funder, appointed 40 percent of the directors and the rest were publicly elected. This created dual lines of accountability and sometimes-conflicting allegiance between the appointed group, which represented very real provincial fiscal constraints and the elected members, who represented the equally urgent public demand for services.

The bylaws of some organizations allow the appointment of 'directors-at-large' who might bring a special skill or perspective to the board. These may or may not be current members of the corporation. In some instances the board, on the recommendation of the nominating committee, makes these appointments. In others, specific constituencies may have the right to recommend, or even nominate, a member to the board. Care should be taken to ensure that the process established for appointment of such directors would result in appointment of persons who can protect the best interests of your organization without being conflicted by other allegiances.

All boards have a secondary legal 'fiduciary' accountability or contractual obligation to funders (e.g., government, taxpayers, foundations or charitable donors). There is a special fiduciary trust when funders have designated monies for a specific purpose.

Boards also carry a moral obligation to the public for the trust vested in them as publicly sanctioned corporations and for expenditure of any public funds they receive. A moral obligation is also owed to consumers or clients, volunteers and staff, as well as other agencies or stakeholders that have a vested interest in the operations of the organization.

The following case illustrates some of the dangers inherent in the operation of appointed boards and reinforces the need for clarity of roles and responsibilities and clear lines of corporate ownership and accountability. It also highlights the pitfalls and pratfalls of pursuing a public policy agenda without due regard for sound practices in governance, project design, management and risk management.

Case Illustration: Ownership, accountability, conflict of interest, risk management

In June 1994, the Cabinet of British Columbia's provincial government announced approval of a 'fast ferries' project intended to improve the efficiency of the province's ferry service and revitalize its shipbuilding industry. The BC Ferries Corporation, a Crown Corporation responsible for implementing public policy and operating the ferry service, was to be responsible for development and management of the project. It created a subsidiary corporation, CFI, to design, construct and deliver three fast ferries.

The complex structure overseeing the B.C. Fast Ferries Project (or 'fiasco' as it came to be known) resulted in real problems in managing the project, assigning responsibility and tracing lines of accountability. Although the Board of BC Ferries was legally responsible for the project, a confusing cast of other players effectively made key decisions. Interference by the Minister responsible for the corporation, appointment of the Minister's preferred candidate for the CEO position, the role of the Crown Corporations Secretariat and Treasury Board, and the Cabinet's overarching authority seriously undermined the board's decision-making autonomy. In fact, the Act that set up BC Ferries lodged authority for most key decisions (e.g., routes, fares, corporate borrowings and capital budgets) in Cabinet or Treasury Board. Although this level of complexity may be peculiar to public/crown corporations, its lessons are instructive for both nonprofits and other corporations with complicated ownership structures.

continued overleaf

continued from previous page

When it was first established, the CFI Board was composed of three outside directors and four senior managers from BC Ferries. Members of the parent board replaced the outside directors in April 1997 when the former began to ask tough questions about the Fast Ferries project. This unchecked conflict of interest and accountability removed any independent checks and balances on the project.

The project was also plagued by a lack of role clarity among the various key players, "insufficient information and analysis to demonstrate that the ferries would meet either BC Ferries' needs or the government's public policy goals in a cost-effective manner," failure to follow sound practices for managing the risks inherent to large capital projects, design flaws, poor reporting on costs and construction progress, serious conflicts of interest between the parent and subsidiary corporations (including a CEO who served both), subordination of the due diligence of board members to political agendas and default in performance monitoring by the boards, central agencies and Cabinet.

Project costs more than double the original estimates, design flaws and project delays cast serious doubt on whether the initial policy objectives would or could be met. Heavy criticism from the public, media and opposition parties was an inevitable consequence, and resulted in loss of credibility for the project, the BC Ferries Corporation and the government itself. The political fallout from the project contributed to the defeat of the provincial New Democratic Party government in the subsequent election.

Post-script: The ferries never operated properly and were eventually sold for approximately $16 million, a loss of some $450 million.

4.3 ORGANIZING FOR ACCOUNTABLE GOVERNANCE

4.3.1 Factors to consider

There are several factors that should be taken into consideration when deciding on an appropriate approach to governance and accountability in the nonprofit organization. The most important are:

- The *board selection process,* which defines legal or 'de jure' ownership of the organization and primary accountability.

- The *form of incorporation* (See Appendix B) and *charitable status,* which prescribe certain accountability mechanisms and reporting requirements.

- The *legislative mandate,* which may define the organization's purpose and mandate and prescribe special responsibilities, such as education or health care, for the board and organization. In the case of school boards, the director of education may have a dual reporting obligation to the board and ministry.

- The *mission* or *'business' and values* of the organization, established by the board of directors within the parameters of the legislative mandate and its articles of incorporation. A particular board type may be called for, depending on mission or values. For example community service clubs tend to depend on operational boards, nonprofits committed to decision-making that fully engages staff and consumers may prefer a collective board, and fundraising organizations may tend toward greater board involvement in operations. (See Part 3.1: Establishing/safeguarding the mission and planning for the future.)

- The *developmental stage* of the organization (whether the organization is in its formational stage, is now incorporated, has newly begun operations, or is in a more mature and established stage with some history of achievements). The demand for board involvement in operational detail is typically much higher during the formative stage of an organization when bylaws and organizational structure are being created. In fact, during the formative stage, boards are often the sole owners of the organization or are much more directly engaged with the ownership base than at subsequent stages.

- *Size and complexity* of the organization. These should be major determinants of appropriate governance practices. Smaller organizations with small operating budgets and few, if any, staff will necessarily demand a greater level of board involvement in operations than organizations with large budgets and staff managed by a senior staff person (e.g., coordinator, executive director, chief executive officer, etc.). Board members of organizations with complex or multiple program areas that call for detailed and often professional knowledge are advised to adopt a results-based governance approach that focuses on board rather than management responsibilities. Smaller organizations with fewer staff and less complicated program structures tend to have less formal structure and processes and fewer resources to develop them. As organizations grow in size and complexity, however, they become more formally structured, and some form of hierarchical management must be introduced in order to make 'management manageable'. This inevitably creates some distance between the board and the staff and clientele of the organization and forces the board to adopt proxy measures of organizational performance rather than relying on direct observation.

- The *financial circumstances* of the organization. These may demand more or less board involvement in securing financial resources and fundraising. Financially stable organizations generally need less board member involvement in financial and fundraising matters, whereas organizations that are struggling financially must depend on more active involvement of board members. Boards that employ a CEO often have a tendency to inappropriately delegate too much of the responsibility for securing financial resources and fundraising to the CEO.

- The *geographic scope* or *jurisdiction* of an organization. This plays an important part in determining appropriate governance practices. It may be more feasible, though not necessarily more advisable, for the board of an organization that serves a small local area to engage more directly in operational details than a board of a national organization that meets less frequently. A high degree of personal commitment or proximity to the organization's headquarters may result in one or two board members being more active in financial, human resources or policy development and advocacy functions. However, board members separated from operational headquarters by long distances are advised to adopt an approach to governance that concentrates use of their limited time on governance rather than management or operational issues.

- *Critical events and transitional phases.* These may demand a different approach to governance, if only temporarily. Greater board involvement in operational detail may be needed to guide an organization through the turbulence caused by sudden departure of a CEO, an imminent financial crisis or other factors discussed in Part 3.7: Management of critical events and transitional phases.

> ### Quick Tip
>
> Serious problems or crises are almost inevitable in boards that do not change their governance practices as their organization grows in size and increases in complexity. Focus on future directions, strategic priorities and key results.

Part Five – Structuring the Board and Committees

5.1 Board structure

It is generally accepted that form (structure) should follow (serve or emanate from) function (responsibilities). This means that a board is likely to add greater value to an organization if it is structured so that it facilitates and guides the work of the organization and its management.

An organization's governance *structure* consists of the legislative framework under which the organization is created (its legal mandate); its incorporation documents; its bylaws; and the governance policies that the board has developed to define how it will carry out its responsibilities and the general rules under which it will operate. This structure includes:

- legislative mandate;
- incorporation documents (e.g., letters patent or articles of incorporation);
- bylaws that define the organization's members, the size of the board, standing committees, the roles of officers and essential governance functions;
- a statement of the organization's mission or purposes;
- job descriptions for the board, individual board members and the senior staff person (executive director or CEO);
- composition and terms of reference of board committees;
- mechanisms for accountability to the organization's 'owners' (voting members), funders and other key stakeholders; and
- governance policies (see Part 8.15 for a more detailed outline):
    - policies governing the interrelationship between the board and staff and the degree of board involvement in management or operational matters;
    - statement of organizational values;
    - code of conduct;
    - conflict of interest policy;
    - rules for management of meetings; and
    - clear role descriptions for the board, board members, committees and executive director to ensure clear lines of authority.

The bylaws of an organization are the fundamental guide for governance of the organization. They express the purpose of the organization; its general objectives; the membership (ownership) structure; how the board is elected; officers and their roles; committees and their roles; procedures for membership meetings; voting protocol; and powers of the board. (See Part 8.14 for further detail on what should be included in the bylaws.)

<table>
<tr><td>

Quick Tips

Clear definition of roles and expectations is as important as how specific responsibilities are divided or shared between the board and executive director, provided that one does not undermine the authority of the other.

Deciding on the appropriate number of board members for your organization is also important. You need enough board members to do the board's work effectively, but too many board members can inhibit participation in discussions and impair effective decision-making.

</td><td>

Case Illustration: Lack of role clarity can lead to problems

The chair of a social service organization that had an executive director and an $8-million budget took up office in the agency headquarters and distributed business cards that identified him as the chief executive officer. This created role confusion for staff and external agencies and conflict with the legitimate titleholder, the executive director, who, in an already tenuous employment relationship, deferred to the chair in the exercise of some of his responsibilities. It also resulted in the turnover of several executive directors and the ultimate takeover of the board by the funding authority.

</td></tr>
</table>

5.2   BOARD COMPOSITION

The bylaws of a corporation must contain criteria that identify who may be eligible to serve on its board of directors and their terms of office. These criteria may include residency requirements, age restrictions (eligibility is usually restricted to adults who are competent to enter contractual relationships) and affiliation requirements (e.g., eligibility may be limited to members with a particular relationship to the cause such as individuals with a specific disease or their family members). They may also restrict board eligibility to members of the corporation or permit 'directors-at-large' (who are not regular members of the organization) either elected by the membership or appointed by the board. The bylaws may also contain other restrictions such as one that empowers the board to disqualify persons whom it "deems to have interests adverse to the interests of the corporation" (such as a recently dismissed employee or a plaintiff conducting a legal action against the corporation).

There may be no law that prohibits an executive director (CEO) or other staff from being eligible to serve on a board. However, good practice advises against this because of the danger of real or apparent conflict of interest and interference with clear lines of accountability. Even publicly traded corporations are moving away from management-dominated boards, either voluntarily or through encouragement from regulatory authorities such as Securities and Exchange Commissions.[55]

The following caution, sounded two decades ago by Stanford University Professor and organizational behaviorist, R. M. Kramer, went largely ignored. "When the executive is elevated to co-equal board membership, has more than advisory power in nominating board members, develops personal relationships with those who must evaluate his/her performance, is permitted to operate independent of board oversight, or can commit agency resources without review, the duty of vigilance has been breached. In such circumstances, the traditional notion of partnership, if it actually exists, has been displaced by one of power/dependency" *in which the executive dominates.* [56]

The nature of the relationship between boards and CEOs is often much more complex than the austere arm's-length one suggested above. In practice, the CEO often develops a friendly relationship with the chair and other board members. However, care should be exercised in development of personal friendships between board members and staff since these might compromise the board's ability to do an objective evaluation of the CEO's performance. It is also important to note, that CEO influence, not control, in the recruitment of board members can increase the likelihood of good teamwork between the board and CEO.

5.2.1 Term limits

It is considered good practice to place limits on the length of time a person can serve on a board. 'Term limits' allow for periodic rejuvenation of the board, prevent an individual or group from developing perpetual control of the organization, facilitate recruitment of people who are unable to make longer-term commitments and provide periodic opportunities for the board to gently ease out members who are not 'pulling their weight'. Terms are typically two to four years, with a maximum of two or three consecutive terms. Incorporation legislation in some jurisdictions may specify the percentage of board terms that must expire each year.

Quick Tips

The overall length of service should typically be no more than six to eight years with some consideration to extend that maximum for an immediate past president during the term of his/her successor. It's also good practice to stagger the terms so that twenty or twenty-five percent of the board members' terms expire each year. This ensures board stability even if the actual turnover rate is higher due to board members departing for other reasons. Term limits should also be placed on executive positions of the board, particularly that of the chair.

5.3 ROLES AND REPORTING RELATIONSHIPS OF OFFICERS

Each of the officers of the corporation is accountable to the body that elects or appoints him or her to the position. In the case of the chair, this may be the board or the membership. Other officers are typically elected or appointed by the board. The chief executive officer of a public sector board may be appointed by a government funding authority (usually in consultation with the board) and, consequently, may carry a dual reporting responsibility to the board and the funding authority. The responsibilities of officers are outlined below. (More specific descriptions of the responsibilities of officers are contained in the sample bylaws and governance policies contained in the CD ROM available with volume purchases of this handbook.)

5.3.1 Board chair

The roles of the chair and CEO in directing the organization are complementary. The CEO's role is to manage staff. The chair's role is to manage the board. Specific responsibilities of the chair include ensuring that:

- the board works effectively as a team;
- a board work plan is developed;
- meeting agendas are focused on board responsibilities;
- meetings are efficiently managed and decision-making is transparent;
- overlap in board/CEO roles is managed constructively;
- directors do not interfere in management (operational, management and collective boards excepted);
- directors comply with board policies;
- conflict of interest issues are addressed sensitively and resolved constructively;
- the board's work and power are evenly distributed among board members;
- board and director self-assessments are conducted;
- board members who fail to meet expectations are gracefully retired; and
- communications and accountability to key stakeholders and the public are adequate.

The chair may be, *ex officio* (by virtue of holding the office), a voting member of all committees, but this is not necessarily a standard practice.

5.3.2   Vice-chair

In addition to assuming the duties of the chair during his/her absence, the vice-chair is responsible for performing other duties prescribed from time to time by the board, coincident to the office. These may include chairing a major committee or task force or leading a strategic planning exercise or community consultation. Good succession planning suggests that, whenever possible, the vice-chair should, assuming motivation and competence for the position, automatically progress to the position of chair.

5.3.3   Treasurer

The treasurer is responsible for the duties prescribed in the bylaws and for monitoring the financial activities of the corporation. These responsibilities are:

- ensuring that complete and accurate records are kept of all of the corporation's financial matters in accordance with Generally Accepted Accounting Principles;
- acting as a signing authority for the corporation as approved in the bylaws or by resolution of the board;
- ensuring that the board is provided with regular reports on the financial position of the corporation;
- recommending a competent auditor to be appointed annually; and
- collaborating with the auditor and executive director in reviewing and presenting annual audited financial statements.

5.3.4   Secretary

The secretary is responsible for the duties prescribed in the bylaws, for ensuring that all secretarial functions are performed for the board and executive committee, and that records are kept of all proceedings and transactions. The secretary is the nominal custodian of the corporate seal and of all official books, papers, records, documents and correspondence of the corporation. The secretary is responsible for ensuring that:

> **Quick Tip**
>
> While the actual authority for performing some of the duties of officers may be delegated, the responsibility for ensuring that these duties are carried out and accountability for them cannot be delegated.

- proper records are kept of meetings, policies, membership and any other records required by law;

- minutes are taken at all regular and special meetings of the board of directors
- copies of minutes and agendas are circulated to board members prior to each meeting; and
- processes are in place for the proper maintenance, security and confidentiality of files and records.

5.3.5   Executive director (chief executive officer or CEO)

The executive director, as chief executive officer of the corporation, is responsible to the board of directors for the administration and enforcement of relevant legislation; for execution of the board's policies and administrative directives; and for planning, organizing, coordinating and managing the corporation's programs and services in a way that is compatible with the pertinent legislation and within the general parameters of the approved annual operating plan and budget. More specifically, the executive director is responsible for:

- generally supporting the board in carrying out its governance functions and responsibilities;
- supporting the board in the development of long-term strategic and annual operating plans and budgets;
- supporting the board in developing the competencies of board members to fulfil their responsibilities;
- providing timely advice to the board regarding any developments that might affect the corporation's capacity to responsibly pursue its objectives;
- managing the corporation's financial and human resources in pursuit of its objectives;
- developing human resources (personnel) policies and recommending these for approval by the board;
- recruiting, developing and managing staff in a manner consistent with approved board policies;
- implementing board policies and directives within the parameters of legislative and regulatory provisions, the organization's bylaws and board policies and directives;
- managing and mitigating risks to the corporation, its clients and board;
- developing information systems and providing reports that allow the board to assess the financial status of the corporation, the general well-being of its workforce, progress in meeting its objectives and compliance with approved policies, statutory and regulatory requirements;
- managing all employee and contractor relationships, consistent with the provisions of applicable legislation, regulations, funder requirements, standards, board policies, contracts and agreements;

- managing the corporation's revenues and expenditures within the parameters of the approved budget;
- representing the corporation positively to the community in general and key stakeholders more specifically; and
- developing and maintaining effective, professional relationships with the board, staff, contractors, funders, other key stakeholders, the media and the public at large.

In practice, the CEO's role varies depending on the nature of the organization, its stage of development and its environment. In some cases, the CEO is a founder whose charisma or personality drives the whole show and without which there would be no organization. In smaller organizations, the senior manager may have front-line supervisory or even operational responsibilities. In other organizations, particularly complex or professional organizations, the CEO possesses so much more information than the board that he or she is not just the humble implementer of the board's grand vision but has to play much more of a leadership role. This places a heavy onus on the board and CEO to work in full partnership while still ensuring that the board has sufficient capacity to fulfill its stewardship and oversight responsibilities.

5.4 CONSIDERING COMMITTEES

Committees have an advisory role. They do not speak or act for the board unless they are given specific authority to do so in the bylaws or are formally delegated by a resolution of the board. If they are delegated to speak for the board, it should be for a limited period of time and for specific purposes. However, the board cannot abdicate its ultimate responsibility for actions taken on its behalf.

Committees do not have any authority to direct staff although they may, through the board, ask the executive director to allocate resources to support committee activities. Collective and management boards are again an obvious exception to this. In practice, if there are comfortable relationships between the executive director and committee members, adequate resources to agree to committee requests for staff support, and no conflicting demands from multiple committees, the process is usually less formal.

Committees should be used judiciously as they can consume valuable board member and staff time. Many boards create too many committees as a means of keeping board members occupied and engaged. The work of these committees often becomes 'busy work', turning board members into "little more than high-powered people engaged in low-level activities."[57]

The chairs of board committees should be members of the board. The only exception is that of advisory *committees* to a board (not to be confused with advisory *boards*: (See Part 2.2:

Overview of board types), which may be chaired by non-board members. The chairs of board committees have the responsibility, in consultation and collaboration with the executive director, for ensuring that the work of the committee proceeds within the terms of reference approved for the committee. Committee chair assignments are an important means of developing board leadership. It may be useful for the board chair, *ex officio*, to be a voting member of all committees. I recommend that the executive director, *ex officio*, be a non-voting member of all committees.

Members of committees may be appointed from outside the board. This distributes the board workload to a broader group and provides opportunities to develop a pool of potential board candidates who already have some orientation to the organization and work of the board.

In general, it is preferable that committees reach their decisions by consensus rather than by majority rule. However, this is not always possible. To be prudent, boards should retain voting control within committees that deal with matters of board policy. This can be done either by ensuring that the majority of committee members are board members and establishing quorum requirements that reflect this or by restricting the right to vote to the board members on the committee. This does not apply to ad hoc 'working' committees that don't deal with board or organizational policy. Board committees should remember that ultimate authority and responsibility for all decisions is vested in the board.

A committee's function is to bring the experience, expertise and judgment of a group of interested and informed individuals to bear on a specific area of the corporation's responsibility. Its job is to assist the board by researching and considering matters referred to it in greater depth than would be possible by the whole board. Committees identify the key issues that require board consideration or corporate attention, propose possible actions, present the implications of these actions and make recommendations to the board, which then makes the ultimate decision. The board does not review matters in the same detail as the committee but must be satisfied that all pertinent information was considered. If it is not satisfied, it must refer the issue back to the committee for further study. The board then considers the committee's recommendations and adopts or amends them or disposes of them in any other manner that it deems advisable.

Working committees have a somewhat different role. They undertake special tasks, such as planning events and fundraisers, conducting research and advising on social policy issues.

The standing committees described below are common in 'traditional' and 'results-based' boards, both of which have a primary focus on governance. The descriptions of their responsibilities that follow can help you develop clear terms of reference for any committees that your board might consider will facilitate its work. The terms of reference that follow can also be adapted for use by other board types. Policy governance boards do not typically use standing committees. (See 7.2 for a summary of committees recommended for results-based boards. More detailed terms of reference are contained in the sample bylaws and governance policies on the CD ROM available with volume purchases of this handbook.)

5.4.1   Executive committee

The executive committee is the board's leadership core. It is chaired by the board chair and is made up of the officers of the corporation, including the executive director as a non-voting member. In the case of boards that have large numbers of directors, the executive committee may also include the chairs of other committees.

The executive committee has specific powers under the bylaws to make decisions between board meetings if unusual circumstances make this necessary. These decisions are normally subject to ratification by the board at its next meeting.

The specific responsibilities of the executive committee in traditional and results-based boards are:

Traditional board	Results-based board
<ul><li>Recruit and select the CEO*.</li><li>Provide general guidance to the CEO.</li><li>Conduct an annual performance evaluation of the CEO*.</li><li>Make recommendations to the board with respect to CEO performance, continuing tenure and compensation*.</li><li>Oversee operations and respond to crises between board meetings.</li></ul> *Many boards create separate ad hoc committees for these tasks. Although the executive committee is often under-used, care must be taken that it does not usurp major board functions or authority and turn to the full board simply to rubber-stamp decisions.*	<ul><li>Recruit and select the CEO.</li><li>Provide general guidance to the CEO.</li><li>Conduct an annual performance evaluation of the CEO.</li><li>Make recommendations to the board with respect to CEO performance, continuing tenure and compensation.</li><li>Respond to crises between board meetings</li><li>Lead strategic planning*.</li><li>Develop an annual work plan for the board</li><li>Make recommendations to the governance committee with respect to the structure and functioning of the board.</li><li>Assist the chair in managing conflicts and complaints concerning directors*.</li></ul>

5.4.2   Nominating or governance committee

The nominating committee (in the case of traditional boards) or governance committee (in the case of results-based boards) is also sometimes referred to as the 'board development' committee. Either the past chair or vice-chair may be the appropriate person to chair this committee. Both tend to have a comprehensive picture of the needs of the board and the organization. The advantage of past chairs is that they may have less of a vested interest in recruiting individuals with whom they have personal relationships. The advantage of vice-chairs, who are in line to assume leadership of the organization, is that chairing the nominating committee allows them to recruit people whom they believe would be a good fit for their future team.

Alternatively, another board member with particular interest or expertise in aspects of this committee's responsibilities may be a good choice. The executive director, *ex officio*, should be a non-voting member with considerable influence, but should not control the committee. The board may annually name other members to the committee. These may include representatives from the general membership of the corporation.

The specific responsibilities of the nominating committee or governance committee are:

Traditional board - nominating committee	Results-based board - governance committee
• Develop and recommend to the board criteria for prospective directors. • Contact prospective candidates to determine their interest. • Identify and recommend, to the board or membership, candidates willing to fill director vacancies. *Note: Many traditional boards have become more sophisticated in their practices than the basic approach suggested here. Others, however, continue to 'scramble' for board members rather than to engage in strategic succession planning, which presents director positions as valuable opportunities for personal development and service to the community.*	• Develop and recommend to the board the skills, experience and diversity criteria for directors necessary to ensure balanced community representation and effective governance. • Identify, interview and check references (criminal reference checks where appropriate) on prospective candidates for vacant positions on the board of directors. • Recommend, to the board or membership, candidates suitable, according to the approved criteria, to fill director vacancies. • Ensure proper orientation, support and continuing education for board members. • Monitor board member attendance. • Conduct an evaluation of the performance of the board and individual directors. • Regularly review the bylaws and governance policies to ensure they are current, and consistent with each other. • Audit compliance with bylaws and governance policies. • Make recommendations to the board with respect to any of these matters.

5.4.3   Finance committee or risk management committee

The board treasurer chairs the finance committee (in the case of a traditional board) or risk management committee (in the case of a results-based board). This committee includes the chief financial officer of the corporation, *ex officio*, in a non-voting capacity. The board annually appoints two (or more) other directors, independent of management, to the committee.

The specific responsibilities of the finance committee and risk management committee are:

Traditional board: finance committee	Results-based board: risk management (or audit) committee
• Generally oversee and ensure development of the annual budget. • Make recommendations to the board for approval of an annual budget. • Review revenue forecasts and expenditure plans presented by management. • Monitor actual revenues and expenditures against the budget forecast and recommend to the board any adjustments that it deems necessary. • Review the annual audited financial statements with the auditor. • Approve policies for financial administration, capital acquisition and asset management. • Review the annual audit statements with the financial auditors. • Recommend approval of audit statements to the annual meeting. • Recommend appointment of the corporate auditor. • Make recommendations to the board with respect to these matters.	• Ensure the development and implementation of a comprehensive risk management program. • Review and recommend annual operating budgets presented by management including items related to staff compensation. • Review financial and human resources management practices and risk management systems to ensure their integrity. • Approve policies for human resource management, financial administration, capital acquisition and asset management. • Monitor trends in revenues and expenditures. • Monitor trends in key human resources areas such as staff attendance and attrition, work related injuries, compensation, staff qualifications, etc. • Monitor compliance with legislative requirements relevant to these matters. • Ensure development of appropriate standards, authorities, policies and procedures in these areas. • Audit or ensure the audit of management compliance with these. • Review the annual audit statements with the financial auditors independent of management. • Recommend approval of the audit statements to the annual meeting. • Recommend appointment of the corporate auditor. • Make recommendations to the board with respect to these matters.

Note: The size of the organization's budget and staff resources determine the extent to which members of a finance committee are directly involved in the actual preparation of budgets and financial reports. Finance committee members in operational and management boards and collectives may be actively involved in preparation of and reporting on budgetary matters and may, in some instances, keep the books and write the checks. The finance committees of organizations with greater staff resources, on the other hand, oversee, review and monitor. Results-based boards use audit or risk management committees that have an auditing/monitoring focus rather than the functions noted for more traditional boards.

5.4.4   Human resources (personnel) committee

The board secretary (or another director) chairs the human resources committee. The board appoints two (or more) other directors to the committee annually. The human resources committee is responsible for overseeing the establishment of general policies for the management of the corporation's staff and volunteers and for monitoring compliance with those policies. In some instances (e.g., in operational and management boards and in boards with a statutory requirement), members of this committee may be more directly engaged in certain human resources functions such as hiring and supervising staff and negotiating staff compensation agreements. (See Part 3.3.3: Dealing with staff, staff associations and unions.)

Note: The functions of this committee may be incorporated into a finance and human resources committee in smaller organizations, and in organizations with collective and management boards. In operational boards, the human resources functions focus on use of volunteer resources. In results-based boards, these functions can be combined in an audit or risk management committee that has the additional responsibility of monitoring trends in key human resources areas, such as staff and volunteer attendance and attrition, work-related injuries and compensation claims, etc. (See 3.4.1: What to monitor.)

5.4.5   Program/services committee or quality assurance committee

The vice-chair (or another director) chairs the program/services committee (in the case of a traditional board) or quality assurance committee (in the case of a results-based board). The board annually appoints two (or more) other directors to the committee.

The specific responsibilities of the program/services committee and quality assurance committee are:

Traditional board - program/services committee	Results-based board - quality assurance committee
• Provide general oversight of the corporation's programs and services. • Receive orientation and reports on the corporation's programs and services. • Monitor the performance of programs and services. • Make recommendations to the board or management in regard to these matters.	• Provide general oversight of the corporation's programs and services. • Ensure the establishment of program, service or practice standards. • Conduct or oversee audits to monitor compliance with such standards. • Ensure that adequate systems exist to measure program performance and evaluate effectiveness in meeting approved objectives. • Generally monitor the performance of programs against approved objectives. • Review client or consumer complaints to ensure that approved procedures and standards have been followed. • Make recommendations to the board or management in regard to these matters.

Note: In smaller organizations, the full board may perform these functions. Results-based boards, however, delegate many of these functions to management but establish a quality assurance committee to audit program performance.

5.4.6 Fundraising committee

Fundraising is a special dimension of the board's responsibility to seek and secure sufficient resources for the organization to adequately finance its operational and capital requirements. Many nonprofit and public sector organizations draw substantial revenue from government sources. Some organizations, particularly those with statutory mandates (e.g., child welfare, education, hospitals, police), may be even more dependent on government funding while others, like religious institutions and service clubs, may receive no revenue from government at all.

Any shortfall in an organization's revenues must be made up through user fees, product sales, investment income, personal and/or corporate charitable donations or other fundraising activities. Smaller organizations that need to raise funds in this manner often establish fundraising committees. If you expect board members to participate in such efforts, it is extremely important to clearly communicate this during the recruitment process because many people are not comfortable with or well suited to fundraising. Most prospective board candidates are motivated by a desire to help the organization's cause in other ways.

Larger organizations with substantial revenue shortfall or capital requirements often establish an arm's-length, nonprofit board to make up the difference. The fundraising board is described in Part 2.2, Table 1 and is discussed in more detail in Appendix A: 8.

5.4.7 Ad hoc committees or task forces

A board may use ad hoc committees, preferably established as task forces, to undertake special, time-limited tasks on its behalf. Some appropriate assignments for ad hoc task forces are undertaking an environmental scan, conducting a survey of constituents, doing a community consultation, overseeing a building project or developing a policy on ethical fundraising or new services to ethnic or other minority groups. Although ad hoc committees can be important resources to the board and management of an organization, care should be exercised to ensure that their mandates do not intrude into areas of management responsibility or usurp management authority. The terms of reference of the task force (i.e., its mandate, composition and deadlines for completing its work and disbanding) need to be clear from the outset.

5.5   BOARD/STAFF RELATIONSHIPS

> **Case Illustration: Inappropriate committee structure leads to board involvement in management**
>
> Parent domination of the board of an Association for Community Living was a large factor in the board's failure to recognize that the Association had outgrown its earlier 'hands on' involvement in operations and management. Use of a traditional committee structure based on operational and management functions encouraged continued board interference in staffing and programming decisions.

My research on Canadian nonprofit boards found that critical events (e.g., financial crises, serious public controversy, labor relations disputes, etc.) and transitional phases (e.g., departure of the CEO, significant board turnover, major budget expansion or contraction, etc.) tended to draw boards into operational or management functions, and that it was often difficult for these boards subsequently to withdraw from hands-on involvement. Transitional phases present a particular dilemma for boards.

Experience suggests that boards that intrude upon key management functions or interfere during crises seriously risk undermining the CEO. Indeed, this has happened in more than one organization that was experiencing serious labor relations problems.

> **Case Illustration: Personal board and staff relationships lead to board involvement in management**
>
> The board of a child welfare agency included municipally appointed directors who were relatives of some of the agency's unionized staff. During a protracted strike, union leadership repeatedly attacked the executive director's management style. As the strike progressed, these attacks became intensely personal. The union leadership and the board members who had relatives on staff called publicly for the executive director's resignation and complained to the funding Ministry about the management of the agency.
>
> The board became badly divided between those who supported the executive director and those who sided with the union. This situation put a serious strain on the organization's relations with its provincial funding agency and the executive director's relationship with a significant minority of her board members. Immediately after the strike, the Ministry commissioned an operational review of the agency.
>
> The executive director remained under enormous pressure from the board for several months before finally precipitating a confidence motion by the board. This motion, narrowly in support of the executive director, allowed her to begin rebuilding her relationship with the union and refocusing the organization's energies on successful program outcomes rather than on 'staff satisfaction'.

Changes on the board (including the chair) and in union leadership subsequently led to a significant positive shift in organizational culture and a renewed focus on delivering high quality services. It also allowed the executive director to make a successful career move two years later, leaving behind a much healthier organization.

Peter Drucker has suggested that a board cannot do its job without meddling, "so it had better be organized to meddle constructively."[58] The results-based governance board has evolved in a way that helps meet this challenge. It acknowledges that there is a legitimate role for boards in operational activities such as the development of public policy. It also legitimizes board activities in support of management or management functions that might be necessary in organizations that are facing critical events or that are in a transitional phase. Results-based governance reorganizes board structure so that the board focuses on clearly defined board responsibilities and on the measurable results of organizational activities and management processes.

5.5.1 Board members as advisors and experts

Board members are often recruited for the specialized expertise they might bring to an organization. In smaller organizations with a less formal culture and less rigid hierarchy, board members often interact informally with staff, particularly management staff. Boards can be a resource pool that is called upon by management for advice or guidance. However, board members must exercise care and tact in offering unsolicited advice that may strain the boundaries between board stewardship and management discretion and authority. Their support to staff or other managers is best provided through, or with the sanction of, the senior manager, regardless of the size of the organization. The senior manager should always be kept in the communications loop between board members and staff so that proper lines of authority and accountability are maintained. In organizations where there is a hierarchical staff structure, it is not advisable for staff to be accountable directly to individual board members or board committees, as this can compromise reporting relationships and undermine senior management authority and accountability.

PART SIX – HOW THE BOARD WORKS: FOUR PILLARS OF EXCELLENCE

How the board conducts its business and the board culture that it develops are as important as the board structure, the manner in which responsibilities are distributed between the board and staff, and other unique characteristics of the organization. Boards will succeed in guiding their organizations to achieve excellent results only if they pay careful attention to:

- board development;
- management of board work and meetings;
- decision-making (how decisions are made); and
- board and organizational culture.

6.1   BOARD DEVELOPMENT

Board development includes:

- recruitment and nominations processes;
- orientation to ensure that directors understand their roles;
- development and use of contracts or letters of agreement for all board members (including confidentiality agreements);
- team-building;
- annual board and director self-assessment;
- minimizing potential for conflicts and conflict of interest in board selection; and
- succession planning.

A survey of 32 nonprofit boards of directors[59] confirms that board members are less satisfied with board development than any other aspect of board functioning. Board members' satisfaction with board development rated significantly lower than 11 other subscales on the Governance Self-Assessment Checklist.

> **Quick Tip**
>
> Boards should set aside resources not only for the ongoing operation of their organizations, but also to support board development and other aspects of the governance function as well as performance evaluation. Funders should be encouraged to recognize this need.

6.1.1   Recruiting and retaining board members

The following suggestions will help you develop an effective board:

- Determine first whether your organization is a community benefit nonprofit, a collective or a producer co-op and what business it is in. (See 3.1: Planning and direction.) The type of organization and the business that it is in will have an influence on the type of people you want on your board and how you will approach governance and decision-making. (See Appendix A: Board types and Appendix B: Organizational forms, board selection and ownership for guidance on this.)
- Understand the importance of a good balance sheet in attracting recruits. Potential board candidates are more likely to be attracted to an organization that is in good financial health than one that is repeatedly in financial trouble.
- Assess what you have to offer prospective board members (potential for contributing to the growth of the organization as well as opportunities for personal growth of board members).
- Communicate clearly your expectations of prospective board members. Put these in writing. Be especially clear on expectations related to fundraising, time commitments, and issues related to director liability.
- Get the right people on the board, i.e., those who will add value to the team effort.
- Ensure a skills/competencies/ motivation fit:
  - As director vacancies occur or are anticipated, the committee responsible for nominations should review the board's need for specific expertise, resources, skills and diversity (e.g., gender, ethnic, racial, disabled, etc.) that will bring strength and balance to the board. The board should approve criteria that reflect these needs. The committee should maintain a file of all candidates who have been proposed or have expressed interest in joining the board, as well as the dates of appointment and expiration of terms of office for current board members.
  - Make sure that your board is reasonably representative of your community and that it has the skills and contacts that will help achieve your goals, but don't sacrifice competence for representativeness.
  - Motives for serving on the board can be altruistic or opportunistic. Appeal to both.
  - Pay attention to board and board/staff chemistry to make sure your team will work well together.

- Ensure continuity and respect for traditions while maintaining responsiveness to the changing context and environment in your community.
- The committee responsible for nominations should identify suitably qualified individuals who are willing to be nominated, check their references, conduct interviews, and recommend their appointment to the board in a manner consistent with the bylaws and governance policies.
- When screening prospective candidates, be vigilant for potential conflicts of interest.
- Develop and maintain an orderly nominations and recruitment process. This will help to build credibility.
- Recruit and evaluate potential new board members (and acquire additional expertise) by including outsiders as members of committees.
- Solicit CEO input to nominations, but retain board control over final decisions.

> **Quick Tips**
>
> Board candidates should be screened for their understanding of and interest in governance as well as their commitment to your cause. Weed out those who want to manage the organization, unless yours is a management, collective or operational board.
>
> More than one person recruited to your board from the same organization can result in conflicts or alliances if their non-board relationships intrude into your boardroom. The same may be said of prospective board candidates who have close personal or business relationships outside of the board. Avoid such potential conflicts as they can stifle free debate and otherwise contribute to unhealthy board dynamics.

6.1.2 Orientation of board members

Ideally, orientation of board members begins during recruitment. Prospective candidates should be given all of the non-confidential information that is contained in the organization's board orientation manual. This will help them to decide if they are interested in serving on your board.

The executive director and the board chair should give all new board members a thorough orientation within one month of joining the board. This should include an orientation manual (see below), a tour of facilities and introduction to key staff. Assigning more experienced board members as a 'buddies' or 'mentors' can help integrate new board members. These mentors can also answer any questions new members may have about board procedures. Remember to offer continuing education to longer-serving board members who may need to learn more about the organization.

Case Illustration: Ineffective orientation

Most of the organizations that participated in the case study research cited in this book experienced difficulties with orientation. For example, one national organization prided itself on its orientation. It was therefore surprised to learn that two new board members who had received extensive orientation just six months earlier couldn't recall having had an orientation at all. Two other board members did not remember that they were expected to give the organization priority in their personal charitable giving.

Your orientation manual should include, but not necessarily be limited to, the following:

- the history, mission and purpose of the organization;
- bylaws and governance policies (including rules of order, code of conduct and conflict of interest policies for board members, if you have these);
- an overview of finances (budget, revenue and expenditure statements, balance sheets, assets and liabilities, cash flow statements);
- an organizational chart showing relationships within the board (committees) and between board, executive director and staff departments;
- role, structure and functions of the board and individual members;
- an overview of key policies and current organizational issues;
- annual report and minutes of most recent board meetings;
- corporate or strategic plan and annual operating plan;
- board work plan;
- executive director's job description and work plan/performance objectives;
- calendar of meetings and events;
- procedural guidelines for board meetings; and
- procedures for board member expenses.

Expectations with respect to meeting attendance, committee work, fundraising and financial contributions should be emphasized. Responsibilities and potential liabilities should also be clearly communicated.

Quick Tips

Orientation should give board members a clear understanding of their governance responsibilities and a general understanding of the organization's mandate and programs. There are several ways to do this. Assign an experienced board member to mentor new recruits. Make orientation a reiterative process, include it as a regular part of board meetings and retreats, adapt it for different learning styles of board members and make continuing education a priority. Use a formal agreement between the organization and prospective board members to make responsibilities and expectations clear. (A sample of such an agreement is provided in Part 8:3.)

6.1.3 Strategies for developing board leadership

Development of effective board leadership requires careful attention to development and maintenance of organizational credibility and recruitment of competent board and organizational leadership. The following suggestions for succession planning and recognition are important elements of a strategy for developing effective board leadership. Some of the suggestions for recognition also apply to developing an effective and motivated workforce.

- Succession planning
  - Include (non-board) community members in committees and events.
  - Assign a mentor or buddy for them and for new board members.
  - Provide good orientation and clearly communicate expectations.
  - Provide continuing education/development opportunities of benefit to the individual as well as the organization.
  - Plan (sequential) succession of board officer positions through to board Chair.
  - Use committee chair assignments to develop future board leadership.
- Recognition
  - Is important for board members, volunteers, donors and outstanding community leaders that support your cause.
  - Don't forget the staff!
  - The most important words are – 'Thank you!'
  - Provide a personal touch that recognizes their unique personalities and contributions.
  - Provide gifts and special awards appropriate to the contribution.
  - Use tributes and testimonials and communicate these in events, newsletters and media.
  - Feed them when you can!

6.2 BOARD MANAGEMENT — MEETINGS, RULES AND STRATEGIES

Strong and effective management of the board is essential to keeping the board focused on governance. This, in turn, helps board members to feel that they are making a valuable contribution and that board meetings are an effective use of their time and talents. While all board members have a responsibility to ensure effective use of the board's time, the board chair has a special responsibility to handle the many potential difficulties inherent in volunteer boards (e.g., discussion dominators, attendance problems, failure to complete tasks, lack of preparation, undermining board solidarity, breach of policies or rules of conduct).

The chair is also responsible for running board meetings. This requires a gentle balance between allowing for a free flow of debate that gives all members a fair opportunity to contribute

> **Quick Tip**
>
> A strong CEO can help compensate for a weak board chair. However, a strong CEO-weak board chair dynamic can tip the power balance in favor of the CEO, erode board accountability and risk a 'blame the CEO' culture when things go wrong. Weakness in both positions is a recipe for unfocused governance and management. When recruiting and planning for succession, look for strength in both positions.

and adhering to proper meeting procedures. The organization's bylaws should stipulate a generally accepted set of procedural rules. These are essential for dealing with board conflicts and with challenges to decisions made by the chair or by the board as a whole. *Robert's Rules of Order* is the best-known set of procedural rules. *Democratic Rules of Order*, is a simpler and more contemporary set of rules. (See Part 8.5 for a brief outline of these.)

6.2.1   Managing the agenda and conducting effective meetings

The agenda for board and committee meetings is an essential tool for managing the conduct of business and ensuring that discussions are focused on matters of board and committee responsibility.

A sample agenda is offered in Part 8.4. Here are some suggestions for developing and managing meeting agendas:

- Provide an opportunity for all board members to suggest agenda items to the board chair, secretary or executive director.
- Have the board chair review and approve the final agenda.
- Ensure that the agenda deals only with matters of governance, which fall within the responsibility of the board, and not operational matters, which fall within the purview of management.
- Make approval of the agenda the first item on the agenda.
- Set 'declaration of conflicts of interest' as the second item on the agenda.
- Divide the agenda into: a) items that require decision; b) simple reports from committees or staff; and, c) general information items that may be subject to requests for clarification rather than debate.
- Structure the agenda so that the most important items are dealt with first. Typically these are items that require an immediate decision or that provide information essential to informed decision making.
- Use 'in-camera' discussions only for those confidential matters where public disclosure might be prejudicial to an individual or to the organization (e.g. information personal to clients, staff or volunteers, discipline of staff, and labor or property negotiations. (See Parts 6.2.4: Confidentiality and 8.6 Sample oath of office and confidentiality agreement.)

- Use a 'consent agenda' to expedite dealing with items that aren't likely to require a lot of discussion. (See Part 8.4: Sample meeting agenda.)
- Assign an estimated time for discussion of each item and use it as a rough guide to the timing for discussions. Set a firm beginning and end time for the meeting.
- If, near the end of the meeting, it appears that more time will be required, seek consensus from board members to extend the meeting. If there isn't agreement to extend the time and/or you will lose quorum, table agenda items you can't get to.
- Circulate the agenda and attachments in time for everybody to read and consider before the meeting.

Here are some additional suggestions for managing meetings effectively:

- Be clear on the rules of conduct for meetings and for making decisions. (See Part 8.5: Rules of order.)
- Suggest, either in the agenda or separately, wording for motions on items that require a decision.
- Require that motions be written and read back to the board to ensure that all members understand what they are voting on.
- Offer an opportunity for each member to speak to each item on the agenda (but don't demand it). Allow a second opportunity for each member to speak if it appears necessary, but ask that they only introduce points that haven't been made before or add support to some that have. Ask the board to vote on whether to allow anyone to speak a third time, especially where discussions tend to be dominated by a minority of directors or time is otherwise limited.
- Use a 'near-consensus' approach to decision-making. In other words, craft motions so that a substantial majority of board members can support them and then call for a pro-forma vote.
- If you're strongly committed to achieving consensus on all items, recruit board members who are committed to long drawn-out meetings.
- Strive to maintain a sense of humor and encourage others to maintain theirs.
- Ensure that responsibility for taking minutes is clearly assigned to the secretary or delegated consistently to the same person in advance and that the minutes include decisions and essential rationales rather than extensive recounting of discussions. Include in the minutes the rationale of those board members who disagree with the majority view and wish their dissent noted.
- Assign responsibility for action on decisions and specify the time frame within which such action is to be concluded.
- Don't repeatedly revisit the same issues on every agenda. Require a two-thirds vote to revisit an issue which has been previously decided.

> **Quick Tip**
>
> If your board members are periodically unable to gather together in the same room, make provisions in your bylaws for teleconferences and electronic meetings. Provincial/state and national organizations, in particular, should consider making use of 'net meeting' or teleconferencing technology.

- Inject some fun and laughter into your meetings! This will encourage attendance and participation in discussions.
- Solicit post-meeting feedback on how well the meeting proceeded and how future meetings might be improved.

> **Quick Tip**
>
> You can monitor the effectiveness of board meetings by appointing a board member or independent observer to monitor meeting proceedings. This person should report back to the board on how much meeting time was spent discussing matters of board responsibility and how much time was spent repeating committee discussions, second-guessing management decisions or reviewing information items that should have been read before the meeting.

6.2.2   A board work plan

A useful tool for the board is a board work plan that is lodged within the broader long-term strategic or corporate plan of the organization. The work plan should be focused on the *board's responsibilities* for the governance of the organization, relevant to the organizational mission and complementary to the strategic and operational plans. This should focus on strengthening governance structures and practices, enhancing accountability, and supporting the strategic direction of the organization. It should conform to the principles outlined for development of 'SMART' objectives. (See Part 3.1.2: Goals, objectives and measurement benchmarks.)

6.2.3   Monitoring board performance

Effective boards are characterized by a willingness to regularly examine their own structures and practices. This type of self-assessment should be a regular component of board practice. All board members should do an annual self-assessment and the chair should assess the contributions of all board members, incorporating feedback from committee chairs. In this way, boards can determine if directors are adding value. The chair should provide a tactful and graceful exit opportunity for those who are not.

When monitoring board performance:

- assess the strengths and weaknesses of your current governance structure and practices;
- determine 'where you are now' (your benchmarks or starting point) in relation to common 'signs of a board in trouble' (see Preface) and 'keys to success' (Part 8.2);
- include a strategy for building on strengths and correcting weaknesses into your board work plan (see 6.2.2);
- use the *Governance Effectiveness Quick Check* (see Appendix C) or the more comprehensive *Governance Self-Assessment Checklist* for board self-evaluation; and
- use a self-assessment tool for individual directors such as that outlined in Part 8.13.

6.2.4   Confidentiality

Respecting confidentiality is not only the cornerstone of trust and confidence, but is also a legislated obligation. At all times, board members must respect the confidentiality of any client names and/or circumstances that might identify clients. Similarly, all matters that the board deals with during in-camera meetings and all matters related to personnel and/or collective bargaining must be held in strictest confidence. This means that directors may not relate these matters to anyone, including immediate family members. The duty of confidentiality continues indefinitely after a director has left the board. Some boards have their members sign an oath of office and confidentiality agreement. A sample is provided in Part 8.6.

6.2.5   Conflict of interest

Conflict of interest should not be confused with interpersonal conflict or disagreements or conflicts over policy, organizational direction or other specific matters. The key things that all board members should understand about 'conflict of interest' are as follows:

- Board members are considered to be in a "conflict of interest" whenever they themselves, members of their family, or any of their business partners or close personal associates, may personally benefit, either directly or indirectly, financially or otherwise, from their position on the board.
- The pecuniary interests of a director's immediate family members or close personal or business associates are also considered to be the pecuniary interests of the director.

- A conflict of interest may be "real," "potential" or "perceived"; the same duty to disclose applies to each.
- Non-pecuniary interests may also present a moral, if not a legal, conflict of interest. This pertains, for example, to a board member of one organization who holds a board or staff position in another organization that may have competing interests. This could place that person in a position of influence or decision-making in conflict with or adverse to the 'interests' of the first organization.
- Full disclosure in itself does not remove a conflict of interest but allows the board to manage its decision-making around the issue.

Quick Tip

Corporations legislation typically requires disclosure of conflict of interest and provides guidance on how this should be managed. (See, for example, the Canada Corporations Act.)

The sample conflict of interest policy outlined in Part 8.7.1 will help you understand, identify and deal with conflict of interest, as will discussion of the case scenarios in Part 8.7.2.

6.2.6   Managing conflicts constructively

Perhaps the most difficult thing for volunteer board members to do is confront board colleagues who may be in conflict of interest, in interpersonal conflict with other directors or pursuing personal/political agendas that may interfere with the organization's best interests. The board chair is responsible for managing the board's conduct. If disruptive influences cannot be resolved through private discussions between the chair and the offending directors, then they need to be addressed by the executive or governance committee or by the whole board. Often the past chair can play a facilitative role. Never assume that such issues are likely to 'go away by themselves'. In fact, they are more likely to lead to an exodus of productive directors and competent senior managers.

Quick Tips

Don't let personal or political agendas interfere with the board's responsibility to serve the overall best interests of the organization.

A director's pursuit of personal or political agendas that are at odds with the best interests of the organization tends to cause board interference in management.

Directors must act in the best interests of the corporation, not in their own interest or in the interests of particular constituencies. This means that directors must set aside self-interest and must perform their duties in a manner that promotes public confidence and trust in the integrity, objectivity and impartiality of the board. Directors of nonprofits typically serve without remuneration and do not receive any profit from their position. They may, however, be reimbursed for reasonable expenses incurred by them in the performance of their duties.

Case Illustration: Board conflict damages an organization

Aggressive board representation of constituent factions and board interference in management created chronic divisions within a native friendship centre. The divisions were so severe that five CEOs were driven out within a period of seven years and all attempts by umbrella organizations to help resolve the conflict ended in failure.

6.2.7   Managing disagreements and interpersonal conflicts constructively

Board members should be recruited with a view to bringing diverse views to board debates and decision-making. In a well-functioning board, constructive disagreements between board members are encouraged. These can generally be managed by following proper rules of procedure and encouraging good listening skills. However, in the heat of debate, disagreements sometimes degenerate into serious conflicts on issues or between personalities. It is important to identify as soon as possible whether such conflicts are based on the issue at hand or have deeper roots based on differences in personal values and history, personalities, personal or political agendas, gender or culture. The first step toward resolving such conflicts is to separate issues from personalities.

The board chair is responsible for managing such conflicts. In cases where the board chair is party to the conflict, a neutral board member or third party should be selected to mediate.

Case Illustration: Personality conflict forces out executive director

The executive director of a native friendship center had maintained her position for 20 years through a combination of competence and cronyism. Over the years, she had arranged for colleagues from other agencies and former loyal staff to be appointed to the board. When the board recruited a long-estranged sibling of the executive director to its ranks, it set the stage for a personalities-based conflict that would inevitably require one or the other of the siblings to leave the organization. In the end, the one who left was the executive director, who had stayed so long in the organization that her detractors outnumbered her supporters.

6.2.8   Managing issues-based conflict

Because of their varied personal and professional experiences, values and expertise, directors bring diverse views to the board's deliberations. There are often legitimate and defensible arguments that can be made for or against various proposals that come before the board. For example, a proposal to introduce or modify a program, run a deficit or embark on a capital campaign can all spark lively debate. These debates may become very animated, particularly when one or more of the directors become emotionally invested in a particular position.

Here are some techniques that you can use to help manage issues-based conflicts:

- Acknowledge the value and importance of divergent views in informing decision-making.
- Practice and encourage good listening skills, understanding and respect. Clarify the ground rules for effective communication: all discussions are confidential; others must be allowed to have their say; participants must listen in order to understand; the whole group 'owns' problems and solutions; the focus must remain on issues rather than on personalities or personal attacks.
- Help the parties to define the issue. State what you understand to be the substance of the issue and seek agreement from both parties on a clear definition of the issue. Name the problem or issue.
- Seek agreement on the objectives, outcomes or decisions sought by placing this item on the board agenda.
- Help the disputants to identify and expand points of agreement.
- Help them to identify why the issue is important to them rather than encouraging more debate on who has the best solution or idea.
- Ask each disputant to 'step into the other's shoes' and 'role play' the debate from the other's perspective.
- Paraphrase or summarize the discussions repeatedly until the disputants have reached consensus on points of agreement and disagreement.
- Encourage both parties and other board members to suggest new insights or compromises. Seek agreement on a compromise.
- Re-state the favored solution. Check with both parties to see if it is acceptable and will allow them to resolve the matter.
- Table the item and deal with it after a 'cooling off' period either later in the meeting, at a future meeting of the board or privately with the parties outside a board meeting.

Adapted from *Designing and Facilitating Groups in Conflict,* Canadian Institute for Conflict Resolution (CICR)

6.2.9 Managing personality-based conflict (dealing with disruptive members)

Here are some techniques for dealing with conflicts based on personality, personal or political agendas, or other more deeply rooted factors:

- Do not waste valuable board time and energy in attempting to resolve such conflicts at the board table.
- Meet with the parties separately outside of board meetings to express concern about the negative effect of their conflict on board deliberations, attempt to define the issues and seek a resolution of the conflict.
- Meet with the parties separately and together to determine whether an accord can be reached between them that will allow the board to function effectively with their continued membership. Seek to mediate their conflicts.
- In the event that such an accord cannot be reached, suggest that either or both parties consider resigning their positions as directors of the corporation.
- In the event that a resignation is not forthcoming, recommend appropriate action to the board that is both respectful of the contributions of these directors and sensitive to their role as volunteers.

These techniques may also be used individually, one-on-one, with board members who dominate or monopolize discussions, disrupt meetings or undermine board solidarity or decisions.

> **Quick Tip**
>
> Address conflicts and conflict of interest directly, tactfully and constructively. Address them with resolve and determination as soon as they appear. Don't let them fester!

6.2.10 Managing conflicts between a board chair/member and executive director

The principles and techniques outlined above can also be used effectively to deal with conflicts between the board chair (or other board members) and the executive director. However, it is essential to first determine if the conflict is 'issue-based', 'personality-based' or arises out of concerns about the performance of the board member or the executive director.

If the board determines that the conflict arises chiefly out of concerns about the conduct of a board member or the board chair then, respectively, the chair or full board is responsible for resolving the conflict using the mediation techniques outlined above or for initiating other appropriate action, up to and including asking the director to leave the board.

If the board determines that the conflict arises out of concerns about the performance of the executive director, and if the executive director is judged to be capable of changing, the board should follow a process of performance coaching and progressive discipline. This gives the executive director a fair opportunity to remedy the performance problem. If the problem cannot be remedied, the stage has been set for requesting a resignation or effecting a termination. Clear performance objectives and regular feedback are necessary to ensure clear expectations and fair process. A process of progressive discipline is critical to managing the risks and potential liabilities associated with terminating an executive director.

If the board determines that the conflict arises out of a serious personality issue or that it has lost confidence in the executive director, it should consider moving quickly to terminate the relationship. In either case, the board should seek legal advice.

6.3   DECISION-MAKING

Boards that are primarily concerned with governance should focus their energy and attention primarily on board responsibilities and strategic priorities. They are advised to:

- base decisions on facts (rather than on opinions) or at least well-researched options when facts are not readily established or agreed;
- strike a balance between firmness and flexibility in decisions that have been made, i.e. stand by decisions that have been made but maintain sufficient flexibility to review those decisions in the light of new information or changing circumstances;
- ensure that decision-making processes are open and transparent;
- provide fair opportunity for all board members to participate in discussions;
- clearly assign responsibilities for follow-up within a specified time; and
- encourage broad-based input to decisions.

Decision-making processes vary from organization to organization. Some organizations go to great lengths to include key stakeholders in decision-making. This is much easier to do in small, informal, limited-constituency organizations, such as founding organizations and collectives, than it is in larger organizations with more complex programming and multiple constituencies. The latter tend to base their decisions on information presented by management and use majority rule.

Decision-making is influenced by how much agreement there is on the consequences and outcomes of a decision. Decisions are relatively easy to make when there is a high degree of certainty (i.e., a strong cause-and-effect relationship between the decision and the outcome) and a high level of agreement about desired outcomes within the board and between the board and stakeholder groups. Decisions become more difficult when, despite a high degree of certainty about likely consequences, there is also a high level of disagreement on what outcomes are desirable. In such circumstances, decision-making relies on political negotiations and compromise. When there is generally strong agreement on values and desired outcomes but less certainty about likely consequences of a decision, decisions must be made based on the best available information.

When there is both a high degree of uncertainty about possible outcomes and a high level of disagreement about preferred outcomes, "traditional methods of planning, visioning and negotiating are insufficient." As a result, boards may avoid the issues, become paralyzed or begin to disintegrate into chaos. Such instances demand creative thinking and reflective, intuitive problem solving. Techniques such as brainstorming and agenda building that sort fact from opinion can be useful. Processes that build trust, a willingness to risk 'muddling through' to uncertain outcomes, and flexibility to adapt decisions as new information becomes available are essential to moving beyond stalemates.[60]

"Leadership involves making choices in the face of uncertainty."[61]

6.3.1   Consensus

Consensus may be defined as 'an opinion held by all or most, or general agreement'. "It does not necessarily mean 100% agreement, but a decision that all can live with and support, some perhaps reluctantly. Consensus decision-making requires participants' commitment to a common set of values, including shared purpose and trust, upon which consensus-based decision-making is founded. It fosters trust by compelling people to figure out creative ways to get everyone's needs met. Consensus also helps build ownership. Each person is a necessary part of the consensus."[62]

The major weakness of this form of decision-making is its potential to generate poorer decisions based on the 'lowest common denominator of agreement'. Consensus-based decision-making requires more time to allow board members to come to agreement and greater skill on the part of the board chair. It may, however, save time later on because there should be significantly less resistance to implementing a decision on which there was consensus.

> **Quick Tip**
>
> Strive for consensus but don't expect 'buy-in' or agreement from everyone all of the time – or even most, of the time.

6.3.2   Near-consensus

Near-consensus is an intermediate approach to decision-making that falls between full consensus and majority rule. It is perhaps the most common form used by nonprofit boards because it requires less time than a full-consensus approach and it avoids the major pitfall of full-consensus. In the near-consensus approach, the board attempts to develop a 'near-consensus' or compromise decision that can be supported by a large majority of the board, even though there may be a small group of vocal dissidents. Once near-consensus has been reached, a pro-forma majority-rule vote is held. This approach requires good skill on the part of the board chair and commitment by members to negotiate a compromise that will enlarge the majority in support of the decision to the maximum extent possible. It may also require more time than the majority-rule approach. However, like the consensus model, it may save time when it comes time to implement the decision.

6.3.3   Majority rule

Majority-rule decisions are often more time-efficient but rely on less direct input from all participants. Majority rule, following informed debate, tends to be the most common approach in voluntary organizations where there is a broad range of issues and great divergence of opinion. It follows the approach entrenched in our democratic processes and constitutional and electoral institutions, and recognizes that there will often be legitimate, irreconcilable differences of opinion in large and diverse groups.

The approach that a particular board takes to decision-making may vary with the critical issues or transitional phases that it must confront from time to time. It may also be heavily influenced by the cultural values and traditions of the dominant group within the organization. For example, feminist organizations, and aboriginal and minority groups may favor consensus-based decision-making, while groups with a deep tradition of representative government tend to lean toward majority rule.

Boards whose members are not publicly elected are more likely to gravitate to consensus or near-consensus decision-making. There are three reasons for this. First, these approaches make board membership attractive to volunteers. Second, they increase the cohesiveness of the board. Third, they increase the chances that directors will maintain a united public front.

6.4   ORGANIZATIONAL CULTURE

Organizational culture may be described as 'the personality of the organization'. It is deeply rooted in the organization's history and traditions. It can be defined as the shared (and often unconscious) assumptions, beliefs, and 'normal behaviors' (norms) of the organization or of the dominant group within it. These shared assumptions, beliefs and behaviors are powerful influences on the way people conduct themselves, on how they define what is 'normal' and on whether and how they sanction those who do not conform. The influences of our own culture and those of the social or work group we inhabit largely determine how we behave. Organizations with competing groups and cultures can become highly conflicted and dysfunctional.

The culture of an organization and the board responsible for its stewardship is an often-overlooked factor contributing to or detracting from effective governance. It may, in fact, be the most important factor. Board culture emanates from and affects the culture within the organization, and vice versa. The two are deeply intertwined.

Some organizations, like individuals, are more open to change than others. Organizational culture, like the personality of an individual, is particularly resistant to change. There is growing recognition that successful organizational change must include changing the corporate culture, and that this is perhaps even more important than changing structures and processes. Changing an organization's culture often requires outside assistance or even wholesale change that may be precipitated by a crisis as noted in the next case illustration.

Case Illustration: Dysfunctional organizational culture

A national organization with provincial and First Nations affiliates became mired in inter-personal and inter-group conflicts that were rooted in the politics of Aboriginal self-government and Quebec separatism. Board and membership decision-making was paralyzed by endless discussions and an inability to find consensus through compromise. The entire organization verged on the brink of disintegration and dissolution. Intervention by external consultants, contracted by the funder, was essential to salvage the organization.

The outside intervention succeeded in creating new bylaws, introducing a new governance structure, retiring the incumbent directors and electing new directors who had not been embroiled in the earlier conflicts. This would not have been possible had the organization not faced the real threat of losing its core funding. The First Nations affiliate withdrew from the organization because its leaders disagreed with the changes. This reduced conflict and paved the way for greater participation from Aboriginal people who were not mired in the past disputes. The relationship with the Quebec affiliate also terminated over irreconcilable differences related to language and financial accountability. However, the outside intervention and redesign of governance structures was essential to the national organization's emergence from the earlier quagmire.

Because organizational culture is made up of explicit values, rules and behavioral norms as well as implicit assumptions and practices that are rooted in organizational tradition and history, it is not easily changed by the imposition of formal rules. Organizational culture comprises everything from approaches to dress codes and coffee breaks, attitudes toward teamwork and collaboration, the degree of openness or transparency in communications and decision-making, the absence or presence of flexibility and adaptability within the organization, through to methods of conflict management and the use of technology. Serious incongruence between explicit statements of values or rules and actual behavior is a sign of an organizational 'split personality'.

How board members and senior managers conduct themselves in relationship to the organization's statement of values and code of conduct (i.e., the degree to which they practice what they preach) has an enormous impact on the organization itself. Leaders lead by example.

The next two sections discuss an approach to the development of an organizational culture in which board, managers, staff and volunteers feel valued, nurtured, supported and encouraged to take measured risks in pursuit of organizational aims. They build upon principles of 'learning organizations' advocated by Peter Senge in his book, *The Fifth Discipline*.[63] They discuss strategies for developing learning organizations and for building organizations that maintain a sound balance between organizational stability and sufficient 'nimbleness' to innovate and adapt to a rapidly changing environment.

6.4.1   Creating a 'safe' learning environment

> **Quick Tip**
>
> Blame, censure and personal criticism can make people retreat into a shell or resort to subterfuge. Work on building team spirit and collegiality. Create opportunities for social interaction between board members, outside of formal meetings to build understanding, empathy and trust. This can include board retreats, shared meals and shared work on, or participation in, special events.

Personal safety and security are among the most basic of human needs. Trust in relationships is essential to developing a sense of personal security. Trust is established through respect, openness and transparent communications and decision-making. It requires that people be free to express their opinions without being subjected to personal criticism, that opinions will be given careful and thoughtful consideration, and that they will be treated as the property of the group rather than of the individual who expressed them.

People, not organizations, learn. People learn best when their personal needs and views are recognized and appreciated and their many roles inside and outside of the organization are respected and valued. Each individual's past history creates a 'personal lens' and 'mental models' through which he or she views issues, makes assumptions about those issues and acts on those assumptions. A safe learning environment that includes open dialogue, reflection and inquiry encourages people to share their personal assumptions and to consider changing those assumptions. This environment is most likely to exist when all board members feel like equals in the decision-making process and when there is constructive resolution of disagreements and conflicts.

> **Quick Tip**
>
> Organizations that promote on the basis of merit instead of cronyism and favoritism encourage feelings of safety, personal recognition and worth among all board members and within the staff.

Boards whose members are joined by a common cause and commitment, and that stay focused on future goals instead of past events are more likely to achieve their goals in a collegial and comfortable environment. Maintaining an outward, results-oriented focus inspires commitment and nurtures a sense of personal safety and willingness to take risks. Personal or political agendas, particularly hidden agendas, are among the most disruptive and destructive forces within any board.

Recent research on innovation in governance identified the attributes common to boards whose members believed they were very successful in governing their organizations. These attributes included (a) a family feeling on the board, (b) a sense of pleasure and fun, (c) an executive director who helped to maintain a culture of learning on the board, (d) careful selection of board members, and (e) receptivity to change in their culture and practice as the organization evolves (or key actors are replaced).[64]

The Gallup survey referred to in Part 3.3 identified role clarity, adequate resources, a good talent/task fit, personal recognition, appreciation of and periodic feedback on personal contributions, opportunities for learning and development, a sense of common interests and a commitment to quality work as components of a positive workplace culture.[65]

The Governance Self-Assessment Checklist identifies respect for organizational norms, interpersonal respect, trust, teamwork, flexibility, innovativeness, enthusiasm for work of the organization, open and constructive communication, and constructive resolution of conflicts as key elements of a positive culture. These factors, as a measure of board and organizational culture, correlated significantly with external observers' ratings of organizational effectiveness.[66]

6.4.2 Maintaining stability and encouraging innovation

In order to maintain a degree of stability in an often rapidly changing and complex environment, organizations need continuity that respects and celebrates past history and accomplishments. Creating an organizational and board culture in which board members, staff and volunteers feel a degree of personal safety and security is essential to maintaining stability and to encouraging innovation. Avoiding a culture of blame, building on strengths and encouraging 'no fault' experimentation and calculated risk-taking best achieve this. It requires a minimalist approach to setting expectations and specifying the means of achieving goals while remaining steadfast in achieving those goals (See 3.1: Establishing/safeguarding the mission and planning for the future). It means controlling for outcomes without controlling means. It requires that the board, management and staff discover lessons from identifying and examining paradoxes and tensions within the organization and its operational systems.

PART SEVEN – GOVERNING FOR RESULTS ESSENTIALS

BOARD FOCUS AND CULTURE

Many boards do well with an informal approach that is grounded in the adage 'start where you are, use what resources you have and do what you can'. However, any organization, regardless of its stage of development, structure or size, can derive added value from a board that cultivates a culture of systematic planning, monitoring and evaluation that is focused on the results it seeks to achieve. And it can do so without investing in the rigorous application of a prescriptive governance model.

A board that is 'governing for results' ensures that the organization has a clear vision and goals with objectives that are as concrete and measurable as possible for the particular organizational context. It concentrates its efforts on areas of board, rather than management, responsibilities – unless, of course, it is an operational, collective or management board. Regardless of board type or organizational form, a more rigorous approach to strategic planning and performance monitoring can enhance its effectiveness in governance.

A board that is 'governing for results' relies heavily on its CEO as a full partner in developing direction and policies but maintains sufficient independence from management to ensure that it can objectively evaluate CEO performance. It clearly delegates to the CEO the responsibility **and** authority for achieving approved objectives. The three basic organizational functions – governance, management and work – are highly integrated, regardless of the size and complexity of the organization.

A board that is 'governing for results' adopts a logical framework for establishing performance benchmarks for the organization, its programs, the CEO **and** the board. It ensures that adequate systems are in place to measure performance, and monitors or audits that performance regularly. It measures and monitors the indicators of goal attainment that matter most to the organization's overall success.

A board that is 'governing for results' ensures that adequate systems are in place to identify and manage real or potential risks, and to conduct audits to assess compliance with legislative requirements, bylaws, governance policies and established standards of practice. It engages stakeholders in planning, ensures that its mission and objectives are clearly communicated, its decision-making processes are transparent and accounts to stakeholders for the results of organizational investments and efforts.

A board that is 'governing for results' must be introspective. It regularly reviews its practices to ensure that it preoccupies itself with the most important issues facing the organization, ensures that it has good information for working on those key issues, maintains good communications with key stakeholders, sets clear expectations and standards for the performance of the board and the organization, and reflects on its own performance to ensure that it is open to innovations in its own practices and adds value to the efforts of management and staff.[67]

A recent article in the Harvard Business Review identified four basic characteristics of board work that matters which fit well with the 'governing for results' approach. "First, the board concerns itself with do-or-die issues central to the institution's success. Second, it is driven by results that are linked to defined timetables. Third, it has clear measures of success. Finally, it requires the engagement of the organization's internal and external constituencies."[68]

7.1   A LOGICAL FRAMEWORK FOR PLANNING AND ASSESSING RESULTS

The following text and schemata provide a basic structure for organizational planning and evaluation. The central premise of this framework hinges on the application of generally accepted criteria for developing SMART objectives, i.e., objectives that are *specific*, *measurable*, *achievable, relevant* to the organization's mission and *achievable* within specified *time* horizons. Objectives are statements that specify desired outputs and outcomes. This framework builds on the approved organizational mission as the anchor for strategic and operational planning in general and outputs and outcomes measurement in particular. It flows logically through the following steps:

1. establishing a clear statement of purpose or goals to provide a context for organizational activities;
2. framing the definition of the problem(s) or need(s) that the organization or project is intended to address;
3. developing SMART objectives with indicators that will permit either qualitative or quantitative measurement or evaluation of whether outputs and outcomes have been achieved;
4. defining objectives clearly to include outputs (or immediate products/results), desired short and long-term outcomes as well as indicators against which success can be evaluated qualitatively and/or measured quantitatively;
5. identifying resources (human and financial) available to pursue achievement of the objectives;
6. identifying constraints (resource, political or other limitations or external influences) which may impair the organization's or project's capacity to achieve desired objectives;

7. designing activities, within the limits of available resources, that are most likely to support the achievement of those objectives (outputs and outcomes);

8. constructing data collection and information management systems that will, within the limits of available resources, best enable evaluation of whether planned outputs and desired outcomes have been achieved;

9. identifying unanticipated secondary impacts from execution of the operational plan or conduct of the project; and

10. establishing regular feedback loops throughout the process to continuously monitor, reevaluate and adapt objectives, activities, outputs and desired outcomes to new information and changing circumstances.

Brief definitions for the terms used in this framework are provided in Parts 3.1.1 to 3.1.3 and are elaborated on in Part 8.11: Evaluating performance. The latter also provides sample applications of this framework for several types of programs or projects.

This logic can be applied systematically to identify any area of board or organizational performance that may be problematic, and to establish objectives for improvement and benchmarks to measure progress. For example, a board may wish to improve its nominations process, its process for compliance audits, its orientation or decision-making practices or its teamwork. It may decide that a review of governance policies or bylaw provisions is due or that a consultation with key stakeholders on the organization's mandate is in order. These may be articulated in a board work plan developed by applying the logical planning framework presented here.

7.1.1   Planning and Evaluation Logic Model

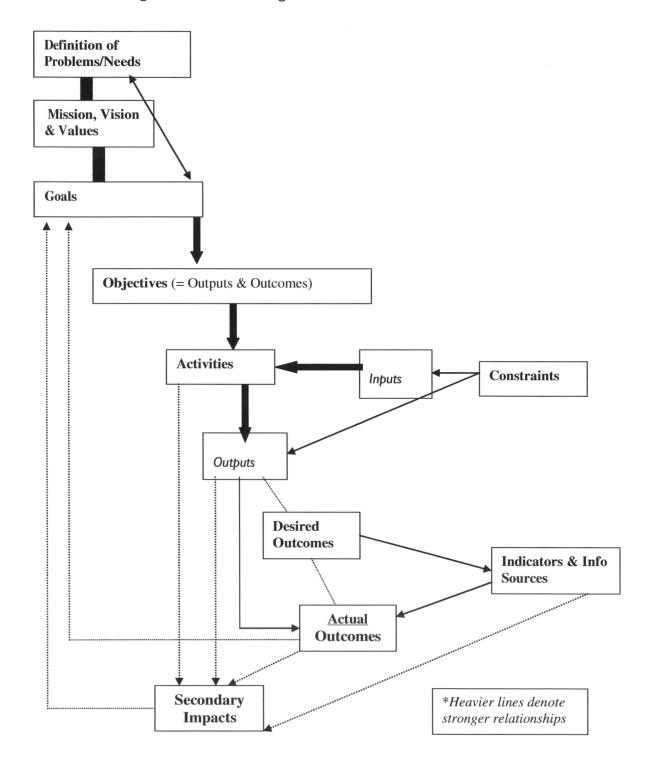

7.2   CORE COMMITTEES FOR RESULTS-BASED BOARDS

For a variety of reasons, a board may establish committees to help it do its work. Certain committees are recommended as part of the core infrastructure of results-based boards. These were described in detail in Parts 5.4.1 to 5.4.3 and 5.4.5 and are summarized here.

Committee	Purpose
Executive	· Recruit, select, evaluate the CEO and review the CEO's compensation. · Provide general guidance to the CEO. · Develop an annual work plan for the board. · Lead strategic planning. · Respond to crises between board meetings. · Assist the chair in managing conflicts among and complaints by directors. · Make recommendations to the governance committee with respect to the structure and functioning of the board.
Governance	· Develop and recommend to the board criteria for new board recruits. · Screen prospective candidates for vacant positions on the board. · Recommend, to the board or membership, suitable candidates, according to the approved criteria, to fill director vacancies. · Ensure proper orientation, support and continuing education for board members. · Monitor board member attendance. · Evaluate the performance of the board and individual directors. · Regularly review the bylaws and governance policies to ensure they are current and consistent with each other. · Audit compliance with bylaws and governance policies.
Risk Management or Audit	· Ensure the development and implementation of a comprehensive risk management program. · Review and recommend annual operating budgets presented by management, including items related to staff compensation. · Review financial and human resources management practices and risk management systems to ensure their integrity. · Approve policies for human resource management and financial administration. · Monitor trends in revenues and expenditures, and key human resources areas. · Monitor compliance with legislative requirements relevant to these matters. · Ensure development of appropriate standards, authorities, policies and procedures in these areas and audit management compliance with these. · Review the annual audit statements with the financial auditors *independent of management* and recommend their approval to the annual meeting. · Recommend appointment of the corporate auditor.
Quality Assurance	· Provide general oversight of the corporation's programs and services. · Ensure the establishment of program, service or practice standards. · Conduct or oversee audits to monitor compliance with such standards. · Ensure that adequate systems exist to assess program performance and evaluate effectiveness in meeting approved objectives. · Generally monitor the performance of programs against approved objectives. · Review client or consumer complaints to ensure that approved procedures and standards have been followed.

7.3   BASIC PREMISE OF GOVERNING FOR RESULTS

The basic premise of governing for results is founded on the following paraphrase of Zen paradoxes:

- If you don't know where you're going – any road will get you there!
- If you don't know your destination – how will you know if or when you've arrived?
- If you don't know where you started from – how will you know if you've made any progress at all?

PART EIGHT – TOOLS TO ASSIST YOU

This section of the book is designed to provide practical tools that can help boards decide which governance practices will best fit their particular organization and strengthen their performance as a governing body. It outlines the factors that may interfere with a board's ability to adopt appropriate governance practices and presents twelve keys to successful governance that were identified through research. It offers a sample letter of agreement for new board members, a sample agenda for board meetings, a sample oath of confidentiality, a sample values statement, sample conflict of interest and donor confidentiality policies, a template for financial monitoring, self-assessment tools for the board and individual directors and a basic guide to 'Rules of Order' for conduct of meetings. It also provides outlines for comprehensive bylaws and governance policies, and references to additional resources.

8.1   IMPEDIMENTS TO THE USE OF SUITABLE GOVERNANCE PRACTICES

Several factors appear to impede the use or adoption of appropriate governance practices. Understanding these factors and discussing how they might operate within your board or organization may help you take steps to protect against them and to adopt practices that will strengthen the performance of your board. These factors are:

- *Organizational history*, which creates a momentum to continue doing things a certain way because 'that's the way they've always been done'. It is often very difficult to break out of established organizational patterns and culture.
- *Lack of knowledge* about good governance practices in general and confusion about alternative approaches to governance in particular.
- *Lack of resources* (e.g., staff and board time, financial) to facilitate development of governance policies.
- *Other priorities* (more pressing issues) that demand attention and time from directors and staff.
- *Personal/political agendas of board members or funders*, which may drive them to interfere in operational details, subvert the majority will of the board with respect to governance of the organization or divert the organization from its primary mission in 'opportunistic' pursuit of funding. This is often referred to as 'mission drift'.

- *A founding board chair or CEO*, who may make it difficult for the board to assert control and establish an appropriate governance role.
- *A board member or chair assuming the CEO role*, which may make it difficult for the board to assert control and establish effective oversight.
- *Conflicts in labor/management, board or board/CEO relationships*, which may impede the use of appropriate governance practices and impair organizational functioning. For example:
  - Board members may tend to get drawn inappropriately into labor/management conflicts.
  - Volunteer board members are often reluctant to deal with conflicts among themselves and often tend to project the responsibility for such conflict onto the CEO.
  - Real conflicts and disagreements between the Board and CEO may inhibit use of appropriate governance practices.

8.2   KEYS TO SUCCESSFUL GOVERNANCE

Understanding the keys to effective governance will guide your board to more effective practices. A recent review of the governance of 20 Canadian nonprofit organizations[69] affirmed that the following characteristics of high performing boards influence strong organizational performance:

- Strong board **and** staff leadership;
- A positive working relationship between the executive director and the board characterized by:
  - Mutual respect;
  - Intellectual flexibility;
  - A willingness to ask and answer tough questions;
  - A clear understanding and respect for the boundaries between staff and board roles; and,
  - A constructive process for dealing with areas of overlap.
- Clarity in the respective roles, relationships and expectations of the board, individual board members and the CEO (*Note: Clarity of roles, and the expectations and motivations that board members bring to them, appeared to be at least as important to good governance and organizational effectiveness as the particular governance approach employed.*);

- A high level of key stakeholder agreement on organizational values, mission and objectives;
- Respect for organizational norms and board decisions; playing by the rules and working as a team;
- Good board development practices (i.e., orientation, training, team-building, sound board member recruitment practices);
- Regular assessment of the effectiveness of board development practices, the performance of the board, its individual members and the CEO;
- Consensus or near-consensus decision-making rather than majority rule;
- A high level of trust and teamwork and a low level of interpersonal and role conflict;
- Constructive confrontation and resolution of conflicts within the board, between the board and CEO and conflicts of interest on the part of board members;
- A good balance between organizational stability and flexibility to adapt to a constantly changing environment; and
- Effective management of meetings and board work (e.g., existence of a board work plan, agendas circulated sufficiently in advance of meetings, board members well prepared, meetings effectively chaired, respect for rules of order, fact-based decision making).

8.3 LETTER OF AGREEMENT FOR NEW BOARD MEMBERS

This sample letter of agreement for prospective board members is intended to serve as the basis of an understanding with new board members that will clearly spell out what they can expect of the organization and what will be expected of them. This letter is intended for use after an interview with the candidate and basic reference checks have been completed. It can be adapted to the needs of any organization.

Dear [Name of Prospective Board Member]:

We're pleased that you're considering joining the board of directors of [name of organization]. This letter will provide you with basic information about our organization, general expectations of board members and what you might expect from us. This will allow you to make an informed decision about your interest in joining our board. Candidates for the board are recommended to the board for approval (or the membership for election at an annual meeting where there may be more candidates nominated than board positions available).

The mission of [name of organization] is [statement of mission]. The board is the legal custodian of the organization and, as such, is responsible for its proper and prudent stewardship. Its role is one of governance. This means ensuring that:

- The organization has a forward-looking vision and a values framework for the conduct of its affairs;
- The mission is respected but remains responsive to contemporary circumstances;
- The organization carries out its business in a professional and ethical manner that is responsive to the broad interests and needs of its members, clients and the community;
- Decisions are made in a clear, timely and transparent manner;
- Resources necessary to achieve its goals and objectives are secured;
- Performance is monitored; and,
- There is proper accounting for performance provided to members, funders, other key stakeholders and the public.

More detailed descriptions of the major responsibilities of the board and of individual directors are appended to this letter.

The purpose of [name of organization] is to [description of core services or programs]. We employ a CEO, [name of CEO], to provide support to the board and manage the day-to-day operations of the agency. We have a staff of [x #], a [year] budget of [$x], and the support of [x #] volunteers.

As a board member, you will be expected to:

- commit sufficient time to become oriented to your responsibilities and the work of the organization;
- regularly attend meetings of the board and of the committee(s) on which you agree to serve (a list of committees and their terms of reference will be provided during orientation);
- review agenda material and be well-prepared for meetings;
- contribute to developing the agendas and to board discussions;
- support board decisions and be a team player;
- provide advice and support to the board chair and CEO;
- attend and/or participate in special events including the annual meeting;
- participate in fundraising (*where applicable*);
- positively promote the work of the organization and advocate for its interests; and
- contribute to the evaluation of the board's performance and your own contributions to it.

You have been invited to join this board because of the unique talents and perspectives that we believe you will bring to the work of the board and our organization. Membership on our board will provide you with an opportunity to serve our community [members, clients] and contribute to its [their] betterment. In addition to the satisfaction you will derive from this, you will have opportunities for personal growth and development associated with new learning, stimulating new contacts, and participation in the democratic processes of a voluntary sector organization that has an important mandate in our community. Although you will not normally have direct contact with staff or clients, you will have a unique view of the results of the organization's work through the board's performance monitoring processes.

Please call me at [phone #] with any questions you may have about the board's role or call [CEO name] at [phone #] with questions about the agency's operations.

Thank you for your interest in our organization. If you decide that you wish to join the board, please confirm by returning a signed copy of this letter to me.

Yours truly,

Governance/Nominations Chair

I understand your expectations of board members and agree to diligently fulfill those duties if my nomination is confirmed. I understand also that my position on the board will be deemed vacant upon my failure to attend three consecutive meetings of the board without good and sufficient cause as determined by the board.

Signature   Date:

8.4   SAMPLE MEETING AGENDA

This sample meeting agenda is based on the principles outlined in Part 6.2.1: Managing the agenda and conducting effective meetings. Several of the items in an agenda may be 'bundled' together as consent items early in the agenda to speed up their disposition with one motion to approve. These should be items that would normally not be subject to debate or controversy. Considering items in the 'Consent Agenda' requires the agreement of all directors. If any director objects to consideration of a particular item in this fashion, it must be moved to the regular agenda.[70]

Name of organization

Meeting of the board (or committee name)

Date, place, time (start and finish)

6:30 pm	Pre-meeting representations, presentations or orientation
7:00	1. Approval of the agenda
7:02	2. Conflict of interest declarations
7:05	3. Approval of or amendments to the minutes of the last meeting
7:10	4. Business arising from the minutes
7:20	5. Committee reports – motion to receive
7:25	6. Business arising from reports
8:00	7. New business (e.g., new program, organizational restructuring, public complaints – each accompanied by a proposed motion)
8:15	8. Management reports and discussion
8:20	9. Information items (motion to receive)
8:25	10. In-camera items and report back to open meeting (e.g. collective bargaining
8:40	guidelines; property negotiations – each accompanied by a proposed motion)
8:45 p.m.	11. Motion to adjourn
	12. Post-meeting debriefing: How did we do? What can we do better next time?

8.5   RULES OF ORDER

The most common rules of order are *Robert's Rules of Order. 'Democratic Rules of Order'* is a simpler alternative that you may prefer. Both are outlined below. You'll also find some useful basic tips about rules in 'Trout's Top Ten'.

8.5.1 The Essentials of Robert's Rules of Order

Robert's Rules of Order provides common rules and procedures for deliberation and debate in order to ensure that the whole membership is on the same footing and speaking the same language. The conduct of *all* business is controlled by the general will of the whole membership; it is the right of the deliberate majority to decide. Complementary to this is the right of at least a strong minority to require the majority to be deliberate, that is, to act according to its considered judgment *after* a full and fair "working through" of the issues involved. *Robert's Rules of Order* provides for constructive and democratic meetings that help, not hinder, the business of the assembly. Under no circumstances should "undue strictness" be allowed to intimidate members or limit full participation.

- The fundamental right of deliberative assemblies requires all questions to be thoroughly discussed before taking action.
- *The assembly rules.* It has the final say on everything. Silence means consent.
- Obtain the floor, i.e., the right to speak, by being the first to stand (raise a hand) when the person speaking has finished; state Mr./Madam Chairman. You must be recognized by the chair before speaking!
- Debate cannot begin until the chair has stated the motion or resolution and asked, "Are you ready for the question?" If no one objects, the chair calls for the vote.
- Before the motion (the question) is stated by the chair, members may suggest modification. The mover can modify as he pleases, or even withdraw the motion without consent of the seconder. If the mover modifies, the seconder can withdraw the second.
- The "immediately pending question" is the last question stated by the Chair.
- The member moving the "immediately pending question" is entitled to preference for the floor.
- No member can speak twice to the same issue until everyone else wishing to speak has spoken to it once.

- All remarks must be directed to the chair. Remarks must be courteous in language and deportment. Avoid personalities, never allude to others by name or to motives.
- The agenda and all committee reports are merely recommendations. When presented to the assembly and the question is stated, debate begins and changes may occur.

The Rules

Point of privilege: Pertains to noise, personal comfort, etc. - may interrupt only if necessary.

Parliamentary inquiry: Inquire as to the correct motion - to accomplish a desired result, or raise a point of order

Point of information: Generally applies to information desired from the speaker, e.g., "I should like to ask the (speaker) a question."

Orders of the day (agenda): A call to adhere to the agenda (a deviation from the agenda requires Suspending the Rules).

Point of order: Infraction of the rules or improper decorum in speaking. Must be raised immediately after the error is made.

Main motion: Brings new business (the next item on the agenda) before the assembly.

Divide the question: Divides a motion into two or more separate motions, each of which must be able to stand on its own.

Consider by paragraph: Adoption of a paper is held until all paragraphs are debated and amended and the entire paper is satisfactory. After all paragraphs are considered, the entire paper is then open to amendment, and paragraphs may be further amended. Any preamble cannot be considered until debate on the body of the paper has ceased.

Amend: Insert or strike out words or paragraphs, or substitute whole paragraphs or resolutions.

Withdraw/modify motion: Applies only after the question is stated; mover can accept an amendment without obtaining the floor.

Commit/refer/recommit to committee: State the committee to receive the question or resolution. If no committee exists, include size of committee desired and method of selecting the members (e.g., election or appointment).

Extend debate: Applies only to the immediately pending question; extends until a certain time or for a certain period of time.

Limit debate: Close debate at a certain time, or limit it to a certain period of time.

Postpone to a certain time: State the time at which the motion or agenda item will be resumed.

Object to consideration: Objection must be stated before discussion or another motion is stated.

Lay on the table: Temporarily suspend further consideration/action on pending question; may be made after the motion to close debate has carried or is pending.

Take from the table: Resume consideration of item previously "laid on the table"; state the motion to take from the table.

Reconsider: Can be made only by one on the prevailing side who has changed position or view.

Postpone indefinitely: Kills the question/resolution for this session.

Previous question: Closes debate, if successful. May use motion to **"close debate"** if preferred.

Informal consideration: Move that the assembly go into **"committee of the whole"**; informal debate ensues as if in committee; this committee may limit number or length of speeches or close debate by other means or by a 2/3 vote. All votes, however, are formal.

Appeal decision of the chair: Appeal for the assembly to decide. Must be made before other business is resumed. It is *not* debatable if it relates to decorum, violation of rules or order of business.

Suspend the rules: Allows a violation of the assembly's own rules (except its constitution); the object of the suspension must be specified.

2/3 Vote vs. Majority Vote

The basic requirement for approval of an action is a majority vote. However, the following situations require a 2/3 stand-up vote for approval. Note that all of these motions rob individuals of their rights. As a compromise between the rights of the individual and the rights of the assembly, a 2/3 vote is necessary to:

1. Modify an Adopted Rule of Order or Agenda
  a. *Amend or Rescind the Constitution, Bylaws, or Agenda*
  b. *Amend or Rescind Something Already Adopted*
  c. *Suspend the Orders of the Day*
  d. *Refuse to Proceed to the Orders of the Day*
  e. *Take up a Question Out of its Order*

2. Prevent the Introduction of a Question for Consideration
3. Modify the Extent of Debate
   a. Limit or Extend Limits of Debate
   b. Call for the Previous Question
4. Close Nominations
5. Repeal an Assignment
   a. Take Away Membership, Directorship or Office
   b. Discharge a Committee
6. Make a Motion a Special Order or Resolution

The presiding officer should take a rising or recorded vote in those motions where a 2/3 vote is required.[71]

8.5.2   Democratic Rules of Order

The principles of *Democratic Rules of Order*

Fairness, i.e., equal rights of members and good order, are the underlying principles.

The **final authority** is the majority of voting members, provided a quorum is present, subject always to any applicable higher law (e.g., a law of the land, a constitution, a bylaw, or an existing standing rule).

In **formal meetings** the chair guides impartially without taking part in discussion. In informal meetings, the chair may participate as an equal member.

A **motion** should be worded affirmatively and must not conflict with any higher law. All motions require a seconder.

The **mover's privilege** allows the mover to reword or withdraw the motion provided there is a seconder and that not more than one member objects.

Amendments can delete, substitute, or add words to a motion on the floor but cannot negate a motion or change its topic. An amendment cannot be amended but may be withdrawn by the mover.

Postponing a motion defers it indefinitely or to a specific future occasion.

Reconsidering a motion allows it to be brought forward for discussion again at an appropriate time.

Referring a motion sends it to a committee for further study.

Rescinding a motion revokes it.

Voting methods include voting ballots, standing, a show of hands, a show of voting cards and voice. For a motion to pass, a quorum must be present and more than half the votes cast must be affirmative. Some motions require a two-thirds majority to pass. (See *Robert's Rules of Order*.)

Informal discussion allows members to consider an idea without the formality of a motion. A motion to informally discuss the item must be made.

Good order stipulates that members should discuss one motion at a time and that a member must not take more than a fair share of floor time or interrupt another member except as allowed with a point of order.

Point of order is called by a member who believes that a law or the meeting's good order is being breached. The chair should allow the member to explain and, if necessary, should call a vote for a decision.

Meeting management and procedural tips

- Discuss the idea together, informally, before forming a motion.
- After a motion is stated, let the mover, aided by the members, modify it before voting. However, if more than one member objects, changes must be made through formal amendments.
- Never allow an amendment to the amendment. The motion can be defeated and stated again if necessary.
- The chair must never allow a member to interrupt a speaker or personally criticize or ridicule another member. [72]

8.5.3   Trout's Top Ten

1. **Don't let the rules get you down.** Many meetings run smoothly with informal use of rules.
2. **Disagree without being disagreeable.**
3. **The chair runs the meeting.** It's important to have a skilled chair who knows how to chair a meeting, not just someone who has seniority or who is taking his or her turn.
4. **Close debate by unanimous consent.** Move the previous question. The motion to close debate requires a 2/3 standing vote. All of this takes time, which you were trying to save by closing debate. Ask the members if it's their desire to close debate. If there is no objection, debate can be closed by unanimous consent without a vote.
5. **Use a counted vote to approve a project.** In a small organization, you may use a voice vote or consensus to make most decisions, but a counted vote can be helpful. If you are planning a project, those members who raise their hands in favor of the motion should be expected to show up and participate in the project.

6. **Voting is important.** Even if a meeting uses informal rules, it is important to ensure that each member's vote is properly counted. For close votes and elections by ballot, you may need someone familiar with parliamentary procedure.

7. **Use a qualified parliamentarian.** In a large meeting or convention, make sure that someone who is not a member of your organization and who knows parliamentary procedure is at the podium to assist the chair.

8. **Use the right parliamentary book for your organization**. If you decide to buy a book on parliamentary procedure, check the rules of order section of your organization's bylaws. If it specifies *Robert's*, get a copy of *Robert's Rules of Order Newly Revised*, 10th Edition, 2000. If it indicates another authority, use it.

9. **Every meeting is a partnership between the leader and the participants.**

10. **Your meeting should enforce the will of the majority while protecting the rights of all members.**[73]

8.6   SAMPLE OATH OF OFFICE AND CONFIDENTIALITY AGREEMENT

An oath of office and confidentiality agreement can be used in conjunction with a letter of agreement (Part 8.3) to reinforce the importance of diligently fulfilling the duties of directors (Part 1.3), acting in the best interests of the corporation and respecting the confidentiality of certain information. This sample can be adapted to the needs of any organization.

I, [*insert name*], a director of the *name of corporation*], declare that, in carrying out my duties as a director, I will:

1. exercise the powers of my office and fulfil my responsibilities in good faith and in the best interests of the corporation;

2. exercise these responsibilities at all times with due diligence, care and skill in a reasonable and prudent manner;

3. respect and support the corporation's bylaws, policies, code of conduct, and decisions of the board and membership;

4. keep confidential all information that I learn about clients, personnel, collective bargaining and any other matters specifically determined by board motion to be matters of confidence, including matters dealt with during in-camera meetings of the board;

5. conduct myself in a spirit of collegiality and respect for the collective decisions of the board and subordinate my personal interests to the best interests of the corporation;

6. immediately declare any personal conflict of interest that may come to my attention; and

7. immediately resign my position as director of the corporation in the event that I, or my colleagues on the board, have concluded that I have breached my 'Oath of Office'.

Signature: *Date:*

8.7   CONFLICT OF INTEREST

Conflicts of interest are among the most difficult issues for any volunteer board of directors to deal with. This is particularly true in smaller organizations that must rely on board members to do some of the organization's basic work, manage its programs, and provide specific expertise, and who may even be beneficiaries of the organization's services. The following sample policy is offered for adoption or adaptation to the specific circumstances of your organization. Also in this section are conflict of interest scenarios that your board may find useful to discuss.

8.7.1   Sample conflict of interest policy

Members of the board of directors shall act at all times in the best interests of the corporation rather than particular interests or constituencies. This means setting aside personal self-interest and performing their duties in transacting the affairs of the corporation in a manner that promotes public confidence and trust in the integrity, objectivity and impartiality of the board. Members of the board shall serve without remuneration. No director shall directly or indirectly receive any profit from his or her position as such, provided that directors may be paid reasonable expenses incurred by them in the performance of their duties. The pecuniary interests of immediate family members or close personal or business associates of a director are considered to be the pecuniary interests of the director.

Definition of conflict of interest
- Board members are considered to be in a "conflict of interest" whenever they themselves, or members of their family, business partners or close personal associates, may personally benefit either directly or indirectly, financially or otherwise, from their position on the Board.
- A conflict of interest may be "real", "potential" or "perceived"; the same duty to disclose applies to each.
- Full disclosure in itself, does not remove a conflict of interest.

Principles for dealing with conflict of interest

- The board member must openly disclose a potential, real or perceived conflict of interest as soon as the issue arises and before the board or its committees deal with the matter at issue.
- If the board member is not certain he/she is in a conflict of interest position, the matter may be brought before the chair, executive committee or board for advice and guidance.
- If there is any question or doubt about the existence of a real or perceived conflict, the board will determine, by vote, if a conflict exists. The person potentially in conflict shall be absent from the discussion and vote.
- It is the responsibility of other board members who are aware of a real, potential or perceived conflict of interest on the part of a fellow board member to raise the issue for clarification, first with the board member and, if still unresolved, with the board chair.
- The board member must abstain from participation in any discussion on the matter, shall not attempt to personally influence the outcome, shall refrain from voting on the matter and, unless otherwise decided by the board, must leave the meeting room for the duration of any such discussion or vote.
- The disclosure and decision as to whether a conflict exists shall be duly recorded in the minutes of the meeting. The time the person left and returned to the meeting shall also be recorded.

8.7.2   Conflict of interest scenarios

The scenarios that follow are provided to stimulate discussion within your board about conflicts of interest that have occurred in other organizations, without directly tackling uncomfortable issues that may apply to your board. Discuss these scenarios within your full board or break into smaller groups that report back to the full board for discussion.

Madeline's wedding story

Madeline has, for some years, been a director of a social service agency in a northern Ontario community with a population of 20,000. The agency's board periodically holds its meetings at a local hotel where out-of-town board members stay when they attend board meetings.

Madeline is planning a wedding for her daughter, who has decided to hold the reception at that same hotel. The hotel manager offers a discounted price because of the past business Madeline's agency has conducted with the hotel.

<u>Discussion</u>

Should Madeline accept the discounted price that has been offered?

Is this a potential or real conflict of interest?

Should she discuss this with her board as a possible conflict?

If she does, what should be the board's disposition of the matter?

Heather's husband

Heather is executive director of a small local agency, which is an affiliate of a national umbrella organization. The agency has a mandate to coordinate services to people with a rare disease and to their families. The number of individuals and families affected by this disease is small and they form a tight-knit group. Although Heather works for the local agency, she was hired and is paid by the national organization and has a dual reporting responsibility to the national executive director and to the board of the local chapter.

Heather's husband is an active member of the local chapter. Some time after Heather obtained her current position her husband was elected to the national board. He is now in line to become chair of the national board.

<u>Discussion</u>

Would this be a conflict of interest for either Heather or her husband?

Should Heather's husband be ineligible to chair the national board, as some members of the board have suggested?

What are some of the potential problems that might occur?

Should Heather resign her current position?

How should her husband conduct himself if he is elected chair of the national board?

How should the national board resolve the matter?

Carolyn's curse

Carolyn has been director of a small social service agency in a minority community for 15 years. She has managed the agency with a fair degree of independence under a series of boards that have not been very active or involved. Although the agency commands a fair amount of respect within the social service network, the minority community is somewhat divided over Carolyn's management. She has been criticized for stacking the board with friends, for recruiting outside the minority community for an important staff position and for implementing security provisions in a new building that have distanced management from other staff and from clients.

Carolyn's stepbrother, from whom she has been estranged (they haven't spoken at all) for the past decade, gets elected to the board. He is identified with the minority community members who think Carolyn has had an important job for too long and isn't doing it to their satisfaction. The stepbrother denies that he has a vendetta against Carolyn but is gradually drawing away her support from other board members.

<u>Discussion</u>

> Is there a conflict of interest here? If not, explain why not.
> If so, how could it have been prevented?
> How should Carolyn handle this?
> How should the board chair (a local business person who thinks Carolyn is
> doing a pretty good job) handle this?

8.8   SAMPLE DONOR CONFIDENTIALITY POLICY

The rights to privacy and confidentiality are becoming an increasing concern of donors solicited for many different causes. Organizations are increasingly expected to have an explicit policy on how they will manage personal information about donors and the history of their financial contributions. This sample policy may be adapted to the needs of any organization.

The [name of organization] is a nationally incorporated registered charity that receives donations and expends them for such purposes within the [name of organization's] mandate as may be designated by donors. The [name of organization] is committed to protecting the privacy of the personal information* of its donors. It respects the rights of donors to have their relationship with the [name of organization] and their contributions to the Society treated with respect and confidentiality. [name of organization] values the trust of those it deals with, and of the public, and recognizes that maintaining this trust requires it to be transparent and accountable in how it treats the information that donors choose to share with it. The [name of organization] will normally share the name and mailing address of its donors with other charitable organizations unless the donor requests that his/her name be withheld from any list that is so shared. In this regard, the [name of organization] will:

1. Inform donors and prospective donors of this policy and their right to confidentiality by posting it on the [name of organization's] Web site and providing a copy to prospective donors upon request.
2. Limit the collection and use of donor history and personal information to only that information necessary for purposes of solicitation, receipt or recognition of donations and donors.

---

* "Personal information is any information that can be used to distinguish, identify or contact a specific individual. This information can include an individual's opinions or beliefs, as well as facts about, or related to, the individual. Exceptions: business contact information and certain publicly available information, such as names, addresses and telephone numbers as published in telephone directories, are not considered personal information. Where an individual uses his or her home contact information as business contact information as well, [name of organization] will consider that the contact information provided is business contact information, and is not therefore subject to protection as personal information." Privacy Policy, Canadian Centre for Philanthropy, www.ccp.ca.

3. Collect and use personal information only for purposes that a reasonable person would consider appropriate in light of the circumstances.

4. Guard against making unwarranted or intrusive inquiries into a donor's or prospective donor's gift history or personal life.

5. Make every reasonable effort to ensure that all personal information collected is complete and accurate.

6. Ensure that donors have the right to see their own donor record and personal information and verify its accuracy or have the information corrected. The [name of organization] will establish a formal process for verification or correction of information and will inform donors of this process.

7. Provide donors, upon receiving a contribution or pledge, with a formal opportunity to express their request for anonymity and to have their names excluded from any list that may be sold, exchanged, rented or otherwise shared with other organizations.

8. Respect requests from donors to maintain their anonymity by ensuring that the [name of organization] does not publish their names, personal information or amounts of their contributions.

9. Ensure that any donor records that are maintained by the [name of organization] will be kept confidential to the greatest extent possible. A donor's right to anonymity will be limited only by legal requirements to disclose or as otherwise authorized in writing by the donor.

10. Carefully safeguard the confidentiality of information that donors or prospects would reasonably expect to be private.

11. Ensure that all online transactions and contributions occur through a safe, private, and secure system that protects the donor's personal information.

12. Develop and enforce terms and conditions under which donor records (including electronic files) may be accessed and by whom.

13. Ensure that access to personal information is based only on the need to deal with the information for the reason(s) for which it was obtained.

14. Require that volunteers and professional staff be discrete in discussing information about donors or prospects and require that such discussions be conducted in a manner that maintains confidentiality.

15. Require employees and volunteers to sign a confidentiality agreement that obligates them to treat any information to which they are privileged during the course of their fundraising efforts as confidential in perpetuity.

16. Ensure that information, including research, about donors or prospects (including electronic files) is stored securely and properly disposed of, to prevent access by unauthorized persons.

17. Routinely update electronic and other security measures to maximize protection of such information.

8.9   Sample values statement

A statement of core values can provide guidance to staff and volunteers with respect to how they conduct the business of the organization and serve as a standard to which consumers and other stakeholders can hold the organization accountable. The sample offered here may be adapted to the unique circumstances of any organization.[74]

"We Care About and for Children and Youth"
We Value:

- The dignity, worth and equality of each individual, regardless of race, cultural or linguistic heritage, religion or gender.
- The family as the primary social institution providing children nurturance, protection, guidance, teaching and links to their culture.
- Communities that support and strengthen the family in its task of raising healthy children to be healthy citizens.
- The right of children, families, and communities to have service providers accountable to them for service quality and financial prudence.
- The commitment and dedication of all who contribute to the work of the Society, and to personal and professional development and growth.
- Continuous improvement in the quality of the Society's services.

8.10   Template for financial monitoring

8.10.1   Statement of revenue and expenses

This sample statement of revenue and expenditures provides information for the current year and a three-year trend analysis. Accounts for individual programs and projects kept in this format should be summed to the total revenue and expenditure statement for the organization overall. Adapt this for revenue and expenditure categories appropriate to your organization. Five and ten-year trend information should be maintained and will also likely be useful for purposes of analysis. Conversion of previous years' financial results into current year constant dollars will let you determine whether you're actually moving ahead or it only seems so. Cash reserves and administrative overhead as a ratio of total budget are also important indicators to monitor. Fixed versus variable cost measures can be extracted from the expenditures reports and are important to monitor as part of a sound risk management program.

Note: This template should be adapted to your puposes with professional accounting advice.

Year and Variance Item	Yr 1 Actual	Yr 2 Actual	Yr 3 Budget Plan	Yr 3 Projected Year-end Actual	% Variance Budget Over Projected + (-)	Yr 3 Budget Plan YTD	Yr 3 Actual YTD	% Variance YTD Plan Over Actual + (-)	% Variance Yr 3 Projected or Actual Over Yr 1 Actual + (-)
Revenue									
Grants									
Contracts									
Fees									
Sales									
Donations									
Investments									
Other									
Total Revenue									
Expenditures									
Salary/Benefits									
Contracts									
Rent/Maintenance									
Utilities									
Communications									
Equipment									
Supplies									
Travel/Accommodation									
Depreciation									
Other									
Total Expenses									
Surplus (Deficit)									
Prior Yr Cumulative Surplus (Deficit)									
Current Cumulative Surplus (Deficit)									

8.10.2   Balance sheet

"The *balance sheet* is a snapshot of the company's financial standing at an instant in time. The balance sheet shows the company's financial position, what it owns (assets) and what it owes (liabilities and net worth). The 'bottom line' of a balance sheet must always balance (i.e., assets = liabilities + net worth). The individual elements of a balance sheet change from day to day and reflect the activities of the company (i.e., changes in bank deposits or cash on hand, accounts receivable, accounts payable, asset acquisitions, etc.).

The liabilities and net worth on the balance sheet represent the company's sources of funds. Liabilities represents a company's obligations to creditors while net worth represents the owner's investment in the company.

Assets, on the other hand, represent the company's use of funds. The company uses cash or other funds provided by creditors or investors to acquire assets. Assets include all the things of

value that are owned or due to the business." (For more information, see *'How to read your balance sheet'* Online Business Women's Center."
http://www.onlinewbc.gov/docs/finance/fs_balsheet1.html. This site also contains helpful definitions of the items that are commonly found in balance sheets. While it is directed to commercial enterprises, it is also useful for nonprofit and public sector organizations.)

A sample balance sheet, sample statement of revenue and expenditure and sample cash flow statement can be found on the VSI (Voluntary Sector Initiative) Web site in "Resources For Accountability and Financial Management in the Voluntary Sector" (2003) Module 3. Financial Management, found at
http://www.vsi-isbc.ca/eng/funding/financial_guide/index.cfm. This site also includes links to other sites that can help you improve accountability.

The workbook *Financial Responsibilities of Not-for-Profit Boards* published by the Muttart Foundation is perhaps the most comprehensive guide on this subject. This 72-page workbook contains detailed guidance for development and understanding financial statements. It is available in print for nominal cost or for free download at www.muttart.org. Workbooks on other topics are also available on this site.

8.11   EVALUATING PERFORMANCE

Evaluating performance against goals and objectives is essential to determining whether an organization is achieving the results it intends. **Performance evaluation** may be described as an attempt to answer questions in four basic areas:

1. *Aim* – Is the organization or program doing the right thing; that is, tackling the right problem? This is generally a subjective judgment in which those with the greatest power make the final decision about what is right and what will be measured.
2. *Economy* – Does the organization or program make use of its resources in the most economical (least wasteful) manner possible? This is an input measure.
3. *Effectiveness* – Is the organization or program effective (successful) in achieving the outputs it intends to generate or outcomes it desires? This is a measure of intended products and benefits.
4. *Efficiency* – Is the organization or program efficient, i.e., does it get the best possible value for money or best possible outcome for the resources available? This is a ratio of inputs to outputs or cost per unit of service or goods produced; or a ratio of inputs to benefit (to the intended client or consumer). Calculating the latter would be an onerous, if not insurmountable, challenge for any nonprofit.

It is important to distinguish between evaluating the effectiveness of a single project or program and evaluating the overall performance of an organization. It is arguably easier to assess the effectiveness of single programs or projects because they tend to have more concrete objectives and it is easier to see whether these have been achieved. The overall effectiveness of an organization is more difficult to assess. One cannot simply add up the results of evaluations of its various programs. As noted earlier, identifying objective measures of organizational effectiveness is usually difficult to do in the nonprofit environment. Moreover, as noted below, outcomes evaluation in nonprofits is still in its infancy and is afflicted with many deficiencies.

Because objective measures are difficult to identify, much of the research on organizational effectiveness has included subjective assessments by different stakeholders or stakeholder groups, who often draw significantly different conclusions about an organization's effectiveness based on their own criteria and personal experience.[75] Herman and Renz developed a simple scale (adapted from an instrument developed by Anne Tsui)[76] that stakeholders could use to assess organizational responsiveness. It was used, along with other measures, to obtain independent ratings of organizational responsiveness. Respondents were asked to indicate on a seven-point scale whether the organization:

- Was performing the way they would like;
- Met their expectations;
- Should be changed in the way it is run.

This subjective assessment of organizational responsiveness was the one scale (variable) in that study that consistently correlated highly with judgments of organizational effectiveness. Organizations judged to be effective based on other measures were viewed as more responsive by various stakeholder groups. The scale also showed high correlations between the ratings of different stakeholder groups, i.e., high inter-rater reliability.

Using a simple scale like this may be a practical way for organizations with limited resources to get some sense of how effective they are perceived to be. In fact, it may produce results that are as reliable as those that use the more rigorous 'rational' model presented here. However, I would argue that using a rational planning model is more likely to generate overall higher levels of satisfaction among stakeholders than ad hoc planning without a logical framework.

Outcomes evaluation can be described as the collection, documentation and analysis of information that describes "what benefit has been created for whom at what cost"[77] by a particular project or initiative and how this relates to the purpose and goals of the organizational sponsor(s). Outcomes evaluation is essential to accountability.

Outcomes evaluation for nonprofit and public sector organizations is still in the early stages of theoretical and methodological development. The guidance provided here should be viewed in this context. According to a United Way of America review, "There are many things outcome measurement does not do. It does not:

- eliminate the need to monitor resources, activities, and outputs;
- tell a program whether it is measuring the right outcomes;
- explain why a program achieved a particular level of outcome;
- prove that the program caused the observed outcomes;
- show, by itself, what to do to improve the outcome; or
- answer the judgment question of whether this is an outcome in which re-sources should be invested."[78]

Consequently, consistent with the advice offered in Part 3.4: Performance monitoring and accountability, performance evaluation in nonprofit and public sector organizations should be kept as simple as possible. That said, the logic model in Part 7.1 and the definitions and examples in the next two subsections will help to add rigor to any performance evaluation that you undertake.

8.11.1   Definitions

The following definitions used in the evaluation framework presented here are adapted from Cutt and Murray,[79] Schacter,[80] the United Way 'Program Outcome Model,[81] and Plantz, et. al.[82] as informed by the author's own experience in program planning and evaluation.

Problems/needs definition is a crucial first step in planning and designing any new organization, project or program. The definition of the problem to be solved, need to be filled or desired state to be achieved is the foundation upon which an organization's mission and goals are built and from which project/program objectives are derived. It is important to assess the relevance of any proposed program to the organization's mission and general goals.

Mission is the organization's reason for existence, i.e., its 'cause', and defines how it will contribute, at least in some small measure, to progress toward that vision; in other words, how it will improve on the current reality or state. The mission succinctly captures the essence or 'spirit' of the organization and provides an umbrella under which the goals are articulated. It is less abstract and idealistic than the vision statement. (See Part 3.1.1)

Goals state the general purposes of the organization; for example, research, education, health promotion, service to members, service to a client or consumer group.

Objectives are more specific statements about desired outputs and outcomes. Objectives should be measurable and related to goals. There may be more than one objective or program related to each goal.

Activities are the work and processes necessary to achieve the project objectives…its outputs and outcomes. "Activities include everything that is done to transform the raw materials into the final product."[83] They are what the program does with its inputs to fulfill the organizational mission or project objectives. These include, but are not limited to, research, interviews and surveys; data analysis; program design; development of reports, policy positions, educational material, etc.; provision of professional advice and services; education and advocacy efforts; organization of meetings, seminars, round table discussions and conferences; coalition building and networking; development of common policy positions and presentation of those positions to policy makers through meetings and hearings; development of content for media campaigns, communiqués and presentations to committees, commissions and hearings; and mentoring.

Inputs are the resources used by a program to carry out the activities necessary to achieve the program objectives. "They are the raw materials of the production process."[84] They include expenses associated with staff salaries and time; consulting services; volunteer time and expenses; facilities; equipment and supplies; research; production of reports and educational material; communications; administrative overhead; and any other costs incurred in carrying out the activities necessary to obtain the planned program outputs and desired outcomes.

Outputs are the direct products of activities as they may be viewed from the perspective of the 'producers' or sponsors of the program or project as the 'finished products'. They are the identifiable (often 'physical' or concrete) immediate results of the activities. They include: written reports, policy positions, communication strategies (including media campaigns), a day of residential care, a specific treatment for an illness, a counseling session, an educational seminar or a training program.

Outcomes may be viewed as benefits for stakeholders or recipients of the program or project as they might be viewed from the perspective of the 'beneficiary'. "They occur outside the production process as a direct or indirect consequence of the output."[85] For example: new knowledge; increased skills; changed attitudes or values; modified behavior; modified policies; improved conditions or altered status for stakeholders. These fall on a continuum from immediate through intermediate to long-term. The extent to which they can be attributed to the program objectives or activities diminishes with the time-lapse between these and the proximate constraints and external variables and influences that may be at play. Outcomes may also be process-oriented. For example, the number of participants in network-building events may be used as proxy indicators measured against pre-established targets or in relationship to historical trends.

Constraints are limitations on activities, outputs and outcomes imposed by laws, regulations, funder priorities and requirements, available financial and human resources, access to decision-makers and the levers of power, competing interests, and similar internal and external influences over which the project sponsor has little or no control.

Indicators are qualitative or quantitative measures of the achievement of an intended or planned output or outcome. An indicator must be "a fair reflection of program performance (and) measure things over which the program (i) has some reasonable degree of control and which (ii) have a logical connection (cause and effect relationship) to the ultimate results."[86] For example, the success of a planned event, research project, media campaign, educational or capacity-building initiative or policy presentation may be evaluated by participant/stakeholder judgment about the relative quality of the product. Numerical indicators may be attached to new partnerships/coalitions, or to the number of constituents/stakeholders served or engaged. New knowledge or skills transferred/acquired, absent objective testing, are more likely to require subjective or anecdotal reporting. While it may be possible to identify specific policy changes, it is more difficult to draw causal links between these and project activities and outputs. The basic question that determines whether a causal relationship exists between an activity and an output (or between an output and an outcome) is 'Would this outcome have been produced in the absence of that particular activity, project or output?'

Cost-benefit or efficiency of a particular project or program is a ratio of inputs to outputs or cost per unit of service or goods produced; or a ratio of inputs to benefit (to the intended client or consumer). It is a measure of whether the project or program achieved the best possible value for money or best possible outcome for the resources available? It may be captured in the answer to the question: What benefits have been provided to whom at what costs. Assessing whether a particular organization has improved its efficiency over time or whether its outputs and outcomes are more efficient than similar organizations may help organizations make best use of their resources.

Cost-benefit can usually only be approximated since it often requires complex analyses of difficult to measure outcomes involving multiple independent variables. The rigor and expense required for such analysis is almost invariably supplanted by more readily accessible values-based and political judgments.

Another major challenge in conducting outcomes evaluation is distinguishing between activities and outputs on one hand and outputs and outcomes on the other. The definition of the need or problem (a state from which change is desired) is the foundation upon which objectives are built. These definitions largely influence whether a particular process or result is an activity, an output or an outcome.

8.11.2 Sample applications of evaluation logic model

The table below demonstrates how objectives and subsequent activities, outputs, outcomes and secondary impacts should flow logically from a stated problem, need or desire.

Problem/Need	Objective	Activities	Output	Outcome	Secondary Effect/Impact
Community hospital needs new medical diagnostic equipment.	Secure new diagnostic equipment.	Raise funds for new equipment. Secure new resources or reallocate existing resources to operate the new equipment.	Funds raised and/or reallocated. New equipment operating.	Improved diagnostic capacity.	Earlier treatment plans and patient recovery. Improved patient health.
The incidence of disease and death in the community is higher than the national average.	Understand causes and develop strategy to reduce incidence.	Research causal factors. Design and implement strategy.	Research report. New health promotion programs, diagnostic & treatment resources.	Reduced incidence of disease and death.	Improved population health and lifestyles.

The following examples may also help you understand the distinctions between activities, outputs and outcomes for different types of projects or programs. They are intended to provide guidance, not to be exhaustive or comprehensive.

Community mental health or social service program

Goals: Improve population mental health. Reduce the incidence of child abuse and neglect.

Objectives: Might include reducing the incidence of mental illness requiring hospitalization; reducing the incidence of suicide; increasing the proportion of children from protection families served in their own homes as opposed to foster care; reducing the incidence of SIDS (Sudden Infant Death Syndrome).

Activities: Might include research, surveys, designing educational material, disseminating material, promoting healthy lifestyles or parenting practices, assessing clients, investigating complaints, counseling, court proceedings.

Outputs: Might include research reports; brochures distributed; lifestyles and parenting skills training; community information sessions or media spots; client assessments, treatments, court orders, discharges or referrals completed.

Outcomes: Might include increased awareness of mental health or parenting issues and greater participation in counseling programs in the short-term; increased community resources and greater treatment compliance in the intermediate-term; and, improved population mental health (reduced incidence of various disorders and suicide) or reduced child abuse and neglect in the longer-term.

Research project

Goal: To improve the overall health of the population.

Objectives: To improve understanding of risk factors for a particular disease; determine the impact of a particular treatment protocol; identify the incidence of illness; develop a profile of community demographics.

Activities: Literature search, surveys, experimental studies, interviews, data analysis, research.

Outputs: Reports, publications, and presentations based on the research, data collection and data analysis; educational programs

Outcomes: New or a broadened base of knowledge, new skills, treatments, behavior or policies in the short-term; reduced incidence of the disease in the intermediate term; and, barring offsetting secondary impacts, improved population health in the long-term.

Advocacy project

Goal: To reduce the incidence of fatalities caused by drunk driving.

Objective: To influence legislators to introduce stricter enforcement and penalties.

Activities: Research; coalition building; development of common policy positions, advocacy/educational strategies and presentation of those positions to policy makers through meetings, development of media campaigns, communiqués and presentations to committees, commissions and hearings.

Outputs: Might include written reports on policy positions; media campaigns, communiqués and presentations.

Outcomes: Might include favorable reception of positions by policy makers in the short-term; changes in policy and driver behavior in the intermediate-term; and changes in the incidence of drunk driving fatalities in the long-term.

Capacity-building project

Goal: To enhance the efficiency and effectiveness of member organizations.

Objectives: To improve the capacity of member organizations in a particular domain (e.g., financial administration, governance, advocacy, personnel management, technology).

Activities: Research, development and design of educational material; mentoring; collaborative ventures.

Outputs: Mentoring partnerships and educational seminars/workshops. These may be evaluated against numerical targets/indicators such as number of partnerships, training events, participants, etc.

Outcomes: Increased independence and improved results achieved by participants.

Fundraising project

Goal: To raise sufficient revenue to purchase a new vehicle for food bank deliveries.

Objectives: To increase net revenues generated from a direct mail campaign.

Activities: Review contents of appeal package, focus groups, redesign of material, culling mailing lists, researching new target audiences, reviewing administrative systems.

Outputs: New direct mail package, revised lists, streamlined administrative systems.

Outcomes: Increased gross revenue, lower overhead ratio, increased net revenue, new vehicle.

8.11.3   A word about The Balanced Score Card

The Balanced Scorecard, developed by Kaplan and Norton,[87] is another approach used by business, public and nonprofit sector organizations to assess organizational performance from four perspectives: learning and innovation, internal operations, customer satisfaction, and finances. It grew out of the dissatisfaction of private sector companies with traditional financial-oriented measures of corporate performance. It helps to align corporate activities and intended outcomes with the organization's mission.

The Balanced Score Card can be used in conjunction with the logical planning and evaluation framework outlined here and adapted to your own organizational context.

Ontario Hospitals have adapted the Balanced Score Card for use in their annual performance evaluation.[88] They assess activities and outcomes in the areas of financial performance, clinical utilization and outcomes, system integration and change, and patient satisfaction. The result is a series of reports known as the Hospital Reports.

8.12   THE BOARD EFFECTIVENESS QUICK-CHECK

The Board Effectiveness Quick Check contains a number of items that have been identified as correlating most significantly with successful governance and organizational effectiveness. It consists of the first 15 of 146 items in the Governance Self-Assessment Checklist (GSAC), which was developed to help boards identify strengths and weaknesses in governance structures and processes, and to suggest priorities for further attention. These factors are drawn from a survey of the research and normative literature on governance of nonprofit organizations, a review of other rating scales and research supporting the validity and reliability of the GSAC.

The results of the Quick Check correlate very highly with those of the overall GSAC. However, it does not provide the finer level of discrimination between governance practices that result from administration of the larger, comprehensive version. The Quick Check can be used to take a snapshot of your board's performance at a particular moment. Take 5 minutes to complete it, have a board member tabulate the results and use it to focus your board's discussion about governance. You'll find the Quick Check in Appendix C. The comprehensive GSAC is available through the author.

8.13   SELF-ASSESSMENT FOR INDIVIDUAL BOARD MEMBERS

The purpose of this self-evaluation checklist is to help individual board members and the board chair assess the 'added value' that they bring to the organization, whether they have met the expectations set by the board when they took their place at the boardroom table and whether they continue to be committed to serving on the board. It should be completed by board members and shared with the chair. An electronic copy of this is contained on the CD ROM available with volume purchases of this book.

Director's Self-Evaluation Checklist

Please answer the following questions by rating your participation on the board according to the following scale: Agree <u>4</u>; Agree Somewhat <u>3</u>; Disagree Somewhat <u>2</u>; Disagree <u>1</u>.

1. I have a good understanding of the bylaws, purpose, policies and programs of this organization as they pertain to my role as a board member. _____
2. I have a good understanding of my role and duties as a board member. _____
3. I understand and respect the distinctions between the governance role of the board and the roles of management and staff. _____
4. I understand the organization's budget and financial statements. _____
5. I seek clarification when necessary to enhance my understanding of the matters noted in items 1 to 4 above. _____
6. I am committed/dedicated to the mission of this organization. _____
7. I have regularly attended meetings of the board and assigned committees. _____
8. I am well prepared for meetings (i.e., have reviewed and considered agenda material). _____
9. I contribute to board and committee discussions to the best of my ability. _____
10. I provide advice to the board (and CEO if there is one) based on my best judgment. _____
11. I base my judgments on the best available objective information/evidence and what I believe to be the best overall interests of the organization. _____
12. I voice any disagreement I might have with board decisions or direction in a constructive manner within the board as decisions are being made. _____
13. I consistently respect and support board decisions made with due diligence. _____
14. I respect and maintain in confidence, matters of a confidential nature. _____
15. I carry out assigned tasks in a timely and effective manner. _____
16. I am diligent in avoiding/declaring real or potential personal conflicts of interest. _____
17. I attend, and/or assist in organizing, special events on behalf of the board, consistent with the expectations for members of this board. _____
18. I represent the board and organization positively to the community. _____
19. I contribute time, talent and/or money, consistent with the expectations for members of this board and my personal capacity. _____
20. I work hard at developing and maintaining a spirit of collegiality and positive interpersonal relationships within the board (and with the CEO if there is one). _____
21. I have found serving on this board to be personally rewarding and fulfilling. _____
22. I am satisfied with my contributions to this organization. _____

Total _____
Total /22 = _____

I have the following suggestions for improving the performance of this board and my capacity to contribute effectively to the board and organization:

_____

_____

_____

I understand that my responses to this Checklist will be used to focus discussions with the chair regarding my past contributions to the board and future role and responsibilities as a director.

Name: _____ Date: _____

Signature: _____ I wish to continue serving: Yes ____ No ____

8.14   BYLAW PROVISIONS OUTLINE

Bylaws should contain these essential elements:

- Name	- Process for removal of Directors
- Corporate Seal	- Annual and Special Meetings of
- Head Office	Members
- Purpose	- Notice of Meetings
- Objectives	- Errors or Omission in Notice
- Membership	- Quorum
- Board of Directors	- Voting
- Powers of Directors	- Minutes
- Remuneration of Directors	- Director Liability
- Officers of the Corporation	- Financial Year
- Duties of Officers	- Execution of Documents
- Executive Committee	- Books and Records
- Governance Committee (including	- Rules and Regulations
nominations responsibilities)	- Borrowing
- Other Committees	- Amendments

More detailed sample bylaws, which can be adapted for your organization, are provided in the CD ROM available with volume purchases of this book.

8.15   GOVERNANCE POLICIES OUTLINE

A comprehensive set of governance policies should cover the following topics:

♦ Style of governance
- Board member authority
- Code of conduct

♦ Board roles and structures
- General responsibilities of the board as a corporate body
- Policies on governance
- Major duties of the board
- Responsibilities of individual directors
- Due diligence

- Oath of confidentiality
- Disposition of complaints and disputes involving directors
- In-camera meetings

♦ Roles of the officers of the corporation
  - President
  - Vice-president
  - Secretary
  - Treasurer
  - Executive director

♦ Committee roles
  - Executive committee
  - Governance committee
  - Audit committee
  - Quality assurance committee
  - Other committees

♦ Planning
  - Planning cycle
  - Long-term business (corporate or strategic) plan
  - Annual operating plan
  - Board work plan
  - Board self-evaluation

♦ The board and clients
  - Contact with clients
  - Appeals process

♦ Board-staff relationships
  - Introduction
  - Parameters of executive authority
  - Communications
  - Delegation to the executive director
  - Appointment of the executive director
  - Evaluation of the executive director
  - Appointment of other senior management staff

More detailed governance policies, which can be adapted for your organization, are provided in the CD ROM available with volume purchases of this book.

8.16   ADDITIONAL RESOURCE REFERENCES

Only those resources familiar to me that provide substantial added value to the governance content of this handbook, or contain supplementary references, are identified here. Many others may be found in links from these websites or in references.

Voluntary Sector Knowledge Network www.vskn.ca

The Voluntary Sector Knowledge Network is the most comprehensive Canadian resource for management assistance for staff and volunteers who lead Canadian nonprofit and voluntary organizations. VSKN will help you find answers to management problems, issues and concerns. It allows you to:

- go directly to the best information on the topic that is available on the 'net' or find the best books and articles;
- talk over and share experiences on the topic with other nonprofit leaders and experts; and
- seek one-on-one help from mentors who have specialized knowledge and experience with the topic.

Topics include: leadership and governance, community and government relations, fundraising, financial management, accountability and evaluation, managing people, and information technology.

Charity Village http://www.charityvillage.com/cv/main.asp

Charity Village® is Canada's super-site for the nonprofit sector — 3,000 pages of news, jobs, information and resources for executives, staffers, donors, and volunteers. It contains a wealth of resources and links for nonprofits and charities including a learning institute, a comprehensive resources section on a variety of topics, job postings, listing of nonprofit organizations by sector, fundraising, advertising, consultants, articles, book reviews and more.

Institute On Governance, Ottawa www.iog.ca

The Institute on Governance site provides advice on governance; learning tools derived from this author's research, which is summarized in "Governance Do's and Don'ts: Practical Lessons from Case Studies On Twenty Canadian Nonprofits" (Gill 2001); and advice for nonprofit governance based on an unpublished paper, "Guide to Good Governance: A New Framework for Understanding and Strengthening Governance." (Gill 2002).

John Hodgson Library, Canadian Centre for Philanthropy (CCP). www.nonprofitscan.ca

The John Hodgson Library seeks to serve the interests of the nonprofit and charitable sector in Canada by collecting, organizing, analyzing, and disseminating information on philanthropy, the nonprofit sector and voluntary action.

The reference collection is the hub of the library's information service. The library houses over 3,000 titles that represent the most current works on philanthropy, voluntary action, civil society, corporate social responsibility, fundraising, capacity-building, public policy and nonprofit research in Canada. It is supported by professional staff and offers free reference services by email, by phone and in person.

The VSI Web Site http://www.vsi-isbc.ca/eng/funding/financial_guide/index.cfm

"Resources for Accountability and Financial Management in the Voluntary Sector" provides organizations with resources, including Web site links, to advance their financial management knowledge and skills and their accountability.

Board Source www.boardsource.com

Board Source is the most comprehensive U. S. -based source for nonprofit management and governance. It contains topic papers, board and nonprofit essentials, frequently asked questions and answers, research and governance in the news.

Boards and Governance Abstracts (1998-2002) http://bsbpa.umkc.edu/mwcnl//research/renz/boards_and_governance.htm

This comprehensive abstracted bibliography of papers and journal articles on nonprofit boards and governance was compiled and prepared by Jill Cook and David Renz (March, 2002, Midwest Center for Nonprofit Leadership, Henry W. Bloch School of Business & Public Administration, University of Missouri, Kansas City)

The Jossey-Bass Handbook of Nonprofit Management and Leadership, (1994, Revised Edition, 2004) Herman, Robert D, ed. and Associates, Jossey-Bass Publishers, San Francisco,

This is a classic reference that provides useful perspectives on nonprofits, key leadership issues, management and evaluation, financial management, and fundraising, and human resource management from recognized experts.

"**Nonprofit Good Practice Guide**." Dorothy A. Johnson Center for Philanthropy and Nonprofit Leadership. Grand Valley State University, Michigan. http://www.nonprofitbasics.org.

This Web site provides an extensive glossary of terms commonly used in nonprofit organizations and a wealth of other information on matters related to effective governance. It provides excellent research resources for foundations and fundraising boards.

Charity Law http://www.charitylaw.ca/

Charity Law, a website developed by Carter and Associates, Barristers, Solicitors and Trade Mark Agents, provides information on legal issues of interest to charities and not-for-profit organizations both in Canada and internationally in the form of articles, seminar materials and newsletters. Regular newsletters include the Charity Law Bulletin and Charity Law Update. You'll find the latest news and analysis related to legislation affecting nonprofits and charities, including a brief on the provisions of the Canada Not-for-Profit Corporations Act.

Perfect Nonprofit Boards: Myths, Paradoxes, and Paradigms (1998) Block, Stephen R., Needham Heights, Simon & Schuster, Massachusetts, (138 pages)

This almost-perfect little book is perhaps the easiest read among many books on governance. It provides a prosaic treatment of issues and refers to a number of 'historical' governance models: traditional, corporate, board-centered and heroic. It promotes an executive director-concerted leadership model. Supported by good research, Block contends that the executive director is the real key to board success. He discusses, in a simple and straightforward manner, formation of boards, directors' responsibilities and liabilities, board and executive director roles and some of the paradoxes inherent to the nonprofit board. He introduces theory to assist in understanding the motivations of board members and how their talents can be exploited, and makes good use of case examples to elucidate some of his points. His treatment of legal and tax issues is specific to U. S. audiences.

APPENDIX A – BOARD TYPES

1. OPERATIONAL BOARD

An operational board is sometimes referred to as a 'working board' because it does the work of the organization that might otherwise be done by staff. The term 'working board' is somewhat pejorative in that it implies that management or governance does not involve 'work'. The operational board is typical of organizations in the founding stage of pre-incorporation through incorporation and into early post-incorporation. It is made up of individuals who are concerned with a particular cause, service or mission. The work of the organization is usually done entirely by volunteers and tends to be dominated primarily by efforts to incorporate, develop bylaws, fix the

> **Primary focus: operations.**
>
> The operational board does the work of the organization as well as governs it. It is typically found in organizations that are in their 'founding' stage and in organizations, such as service clubs, that have no staff and that must rely largely on board members and other volunteers to achieve their aims. Operational boards are also management boards but are distinguished from the latter by their lack of staff support.

purpose and direction of the organization, establish its structure and secure initial operating resources. There may also be some initial activities such as advocacy, mutual support, fundraising and community profiling to establish an identity.

Staff (if there is any) is usually part-time or temporary and is funded by charitable or project revenue or seconded from other organizations. Legal work may be done pro bono. Volunteers or organizations sympathetic to the cause may donate other items.

Volunteers function as the governance board and perform all of the key operational and general management functions (e.g., strategic planning, service provision, advocacy, securing financial and volunteer human resources, keeping of accounts and records) with no staff support. This is most common in newer, smaller and collective organizations. Operational boards are typically self-selected and or self-regenerating.

Board members create the vision for the organization and partner in its implementation. The board sets policies and general direction. Financial and human resource decision-making is vested in the board. The organization may acquire limited staff resources as the organization matures. Board members act as both volunteer recruiters and direct-service volunteers. Committees support the work of the board. Board and staff, if any, may both be involved in the organization's community relations. As more regular staff is acquired, the board's functions begin to shift from doing all of the work to managing some of it through staff.

This type of board generally works well only in emerging organizations or those that have stabilized at a relatively small size. It usually evolves out of a strongly shared commitment to a single purpose, mutual support or self-help need or community benefit, e.g. disease specific organizations, smaller consumer co-operatives (e.g., day care, housing, food co-ops), sports, arts, cultural and environmental groups, and service clubs. Some grow out of informal grass-roots advocacy groups. Many services for developmentally handicapped children, for example, grew out of parent mutual support groups.

Some founding boards may be established by special purpose legislation (e.g., Regional Health Authorities, Ontario Community Care Access Centers, Crown Corporations, etc.). In these cases, the board has a pre-established mission and access to a much richer resource pool to support the initial phases of its work. This allows it to move quickly to governance practices suitable for larger organizations, particularly if the funding authorities have provided governance templates that individual organizations may adapt to their own circumstances.

2. COLLECTIVE BOARD

> **Primary focus: operations/inclusive decision-making processes.**
>
> The board and staff are involved in 'single team' decision-making about governance and the work of the organization. Board members may be involved in some of the work of the organization, in either services or management functions or both. Boards of collectives govern on the basis of specific values related to decision-making.

Like operational boards, collective boards generally work well only in emerging organizations or in those that have stabilized at a relatively small size. They usually evolve out of a strongly shared commitment to a particular 'values set' associated with a single cause, mutual support or self-help need. The most common examples are single-issue groups such as women's shelters, addiction treatment facilities, smaller consumer co-operatives (e.g., day care, housing, food co-ops), some religious groups, etc. Many of these organizations also grow out of informal grassroots advocacy or causes.

Primary characteristics of collectives:

- Power is shared between the board and staff and sometimes with clients.
- There is equal de facto participation in consensus decision-making, even though legal responsibilities are vested in a formal board.
- Volunteers who perform staff functions in the formative stages of the formal organization typically recruit the board.

- Board and staff have shared values about personal responsibility and control, organizational purpose, and group or collective accountability.
- Screening and acculturation processes for new members are rigorous; the group as a whole participates in screening and approval.
- Strongly inclusive group dynamics encourage team spirit and interpersonal support.
- The group as a whole is accountable for group decisions
- Leadership and rotation of administrative tasks is shared, either nominally or actually.
- Salary parity exists among all staff, including the nominal 'leader'.

Collective boards are vulnerable to crisis or collapse in the face of a values clash within the board and/or staff; when faced with legal/financial accountability or service issues that challenge the organizational culture, or as a result of intractable inter-personal conflicts. It is a difficult, if not impossible, approach to maintain as an organization grows and more formal structures become necessary to organize the work, secure community financial support and ensure proper accountability to funders. They may, however, be maintained with clear rules on how all parties will be consulted and how differences will be resolved. Certain worker cooperatives manage to remain collectives this way.

3. Management board

The management board manages operations. The organization has staff and may or may not have a senior staff coordinator. Committees are established along functional lines, i.e., finance, personnel, nominating, strategic planning, services, public relations, fund-raising, etc. Volunteer directors, as committee chairs, manage and direct operations in these areas.

> *Primary focus: management of operations.*
>
> The board manages operations but may have a staff coordinator. Board members actively manage finances, personnel, service delivery, etc. Staff reports to board member managers directly through a staff coordinator or through a dual reporting line.

Staff, board and other volunteers perform service functions. Board members lead strategic and operational planning and grievance or conflict resolution processes. If there is a senior staff coordinator or manager, that individual is clearly in a role subordinate to that of the volunteer 'managers'.

4. CONSTITUENT REPRESENTATIONAL BOARD

Primary focus: constituent interests.

This type of board is responsible for balancing the best interests of the overall organization against the interests of its constituents. It is typical of publicly elected bodies, federations and other constituency-elected boards. It may, as in the case of publicly elected bodies, have grievance-resolution or ombudsman functions. It may also, as in the case of school boards, have prescribed responsibilities for public consultation and human resources. This approach to governance may also be an element in other board types.

Constituent representation is a system of governance employed by publicly elected bodies, federations or constituency-elected boards that have a primary responsibility to balance the interests of constituents with the best interests of the overall organization. However, when board members have a strong interest in re-election, they may favor constituent interests over the larger interests of the organization.

These boards may, as in the case of publicly elected bodies, have grievance-resolution or ombudsman-like functions. They may also, as in the case of school boards, have prescribed responsibilities for public consultation and human resources.

The selection process for publicly, or constituency-elected, boards is likely to have a strong influence on their role: the extent to which they are involved in a mix of policy, management and operational functions. These boards are more likely to make wide use of board committees and advisory mechanisms; have highly developed mechanisms for accountability to their electors; and make decisions by majority rule. They are also at greater risk of difficult and tension-filled relationships within the board or between the board and the CEO.

5. TRADITIONAL BOARD

Primary focus: governance.

The board governs and oversees operations through committees but delegates the management functions to the CEO. Committees are used to process information for the board and sometimes do the work of the board. The CEO may have a primary reporting relationship to the board *through the chair*.

The traditional board is perhaps the most common board type historically used in the voluntary sector. The board, often through extensive use of committees and ad hoc task forces, periodically drifts into operational matters, particularly in the areas of programs, finances and human resources.

Committees are used to process information for the board and sometimes do the work of the board. Committees are established typically to parallel management functions, i.e., finance, personnel, programs, public relations, etc. They serve primarily as a conduit for passing information to the board, reviewing staff recommendations and providing 'community' feedback for consideration of the CEO and staff. Other staff and volunteers may serve on some of these committees. When the committees do work on behalf of the board, this work is often reconsidered at board meetings.

Committees rely extensively on the support of staff. Committee chairs are often members of the executive committee.

6.   RESULTS-BASED (OR AUDIT/OVERSIGHT) BOARD

The results-based board ensures that the organization has a clear vision and goals with objectives that are as concrete and measurable as possible for the particular organizational context. It relies heavily on its CEO as a full partner in the development of direction and policies; clearly delegates to the CEO the responsibility *and authority* for achieving approved objectives; establishes performance benchmarks for the organization, its programs or services, the CEO *and* the board; ensures that adequate systems are in place to measure performance; and monitors or audits that performance regularly. It ensures that adequate systems are in place to manage real and potential risks and that audits are conducted to assess compliance with legislative requirements, by-laws, governance policies and established standards of practice. Although it works in full partnership with the CEO, the board maintains sufficient independence to ensure that it can objectively evaluate CEO performance. It ensures that its mission and objectives are clearly communicated to stakeholders, that its decision-making processes are transparent, and that it accounts to stakeholders for the results of organizational investments and efforts.

> **Primary focus: governance.**
>
> This board type is focused on setting a clear direction for the organization and getting the best results for the money invested. The CEO is a non-voting member of the board, carries substantial influence over policy-making, is viewed as a full partner with the board and has a relatively free hand at managing to achieve objectives established by the board. Committees are used for monitoring/auditing performance of the board, CEO and organization. Board members are selected for community representativeness, commitment to the organization's purpose, and unique perspective or expertise.

7. POLICY GOVERNANCE BOARD (CARVER MODEL)

Primary focus: governance.

The board governs through policies that establish organizational aims ("ends"); governance approaches or processes; management limitations; and that define the board/CEO relationship. The CEO has broad freedom to determine the "means" that will be implemented to achieve organizational aims. The CEO reports to the full board. The board does not use committees but may use task teams to assist it in specific aspects of its work.

The Board governs through policies that establish:

- organizational aims ('ends');
- governance processes or approach;
- executive (management) limitations, and
- board/CEO relationship.

It is the board's responsibility to define desired 'ends' or outcomes (mission and objectives) and the CEO's responsibility to define and implement the 'means' for achieving these within the parameters of the 'executive limitations' set by the board. The board is responsible for establishing limitations on management authority and for defining the governing process itself (board structure and processes). It does this by establishing policies "because policies permeate and dominate all aspects of organizational life (and) present the most powerful lever for the exercise of leadership."[89]

This approach is commonly referred to as the 'Carver model'. Volunteer board members set organizational mission, direction and general policies governing operations. This approach advocates that boards focus their attention on "what human needs are (to be) satisfied, for whom, and at what cost."[90] The board, rather than the CEO, leads this process.

The CEO reports to the whole board. Only the full board provides direction. The board "speaks with one voice" in its direction to the CEO and on all other matters within its areas of responsibility. The CEO has broad freedom to determine the 'means' that will be used to achieve organizational 'ends'. All operational matters are delegated to the CEO. The board monitors and holds the CEO accountable for compliance with its policies.

The board is discouraged from use of standing committees but may use task teams to assist in specific aspects of its work.

8. FUNDRAISING BOARD

These boards, more commonly referred to as 'foundations' in Canada, are incorporated separately and at varying degrees of 'arm's-length' from their beneficiary charities. A fundraising board may have characteristics of operational and/or management boards as noted in Part 2.2, Figure 4. While they have responsibility for the governance of the organization, their primary focus is on raising funds to support charitable causes. Members become directly involved in various aspects of fundraising. They are expected to make personal donations, obtain donations from others, facilitate access to individual and corporate donors, assist in organizing and participate in special events, direct mail campaigns, product promotions or ticket sales and use their networks to support such efforts.

> *Primary focus: fundraising activities.*
>
> This is typically a self-regenerating board that recruits high profile community leaders for their capacity to generate funds through personal donations, contacts with potential donors or their organizational skills. Its focus is typically on getting the job done rather than on governance. This board type may also be operational if it has no staff; management if it has few staff; or more focused on governance if it has a substantial staff complement.

They are, in this sense, operational and/or management in nature although they may have staff to support and coordinate their activities. They govern by setting direction and strategies and providing general oversight of staff activities, finances and allocations. Fundraising boards with a large staff complement may have less direct involvement in operations. Those with an executive director should delegate management responsibilities to that person although board members, as committee chairs, may be assigned responsibility for managing certain aspects of fundraising.

This type of board may also be operational if the organization has no staff; management if it has few staff; or more focused on governance if it has a substantial staff complement. It is unlikely to share many traits with collective, constituent representational or advisory boards. In any case, its primary focus is fundraising.

9. ADVISORY BOARD

A legally incorporated board that functions in an advisory mode is often referred to as a 'rubber-stamp' board that is under the effective control of the CEO. Boards that function in this manner have the potential to create serious personal liability for their members. The risk

> *Primary focus: advice and contacts.*
>
> This type of board is CEO selected and dominated. It provides prima facie legitimacy to the organization but governs only in a nominal sense. Board members are selected for community profile and contacts and essentially provide advice and rubber-stamp CEO recommended budget and plans with little, if any, monitoring of activities except through receipt of periodic reports.

increases with the degree to which the organization's activities expose it to potential civil or criminal liability emanating from the failure of staff, management or board members to exercise due diligence in the performance of their duties.

This board type is not recommended as a model for governance of an independent organization. Unfortunately, many boards fall into this model by default, either by abdicating their governance responsibilities through excessive reliance on a CEO or by allowing a powerful CEO to usurp those responsibilities.

There is a legitimate role for advisory committees. They may be used as a vehicle to provide a voice to citizens or to provide 'advice and oversight' to programs in arts, recreation and other aspects of community services. The advisory board is a key element in the structure of certain religious institutions.

Use of the terms 'advisory' and 'governance' interchangeably can create serious role confusion for board members. An advisory committee has only those responsibilities that are delegated to it by the legally constituted board or council of an organization or institution. It has no legal authority other than that vested in and exercised by its 'parent' board.

Appendix B – Organizational Forms, Board Selection and Ownership

The form (or structure) of an incorporated organization is defined by the legislation under which it is incorporated and its incorporation documents or constitution. These describe its purposes, its membership, how the board is selected (its ownership structure) and how it is governed.

Ownership structure may also be influenced by the stage it is at in its incorporation process (.e.g. founding stage) and its underpinning values (e.g. collectives and cooperatives). Certain organizational forms (e.g. collectives and constituent-representational) may also be classified as board types as discussed in Part 2.2. (See also Part 4.1 and 4.2) The most common organizational forms are identified here.

The founding stage of an organization is the early start-up phase that in many organizations leads to and includes incorporation. Its board usually consists of a group of individuals that is concerned with a particular cause or service and that has been brought together by that common cause. The board is constituted through self-selection based on consensus of the active group. It is sometimes referred to as a formative board although it is, in this categorization, not an organizational form but an operational board. Its initial 'ownership' is vested primarily in the founding members who sign the incorporation documents. However, it may ultimately take on any of the organizational forms and use any of the board selection methods described in this appendix.

A. Collective

This is both an organizational form and a board type (See Appendix A: Board types). The board and staff form a 'single team' to make decisions about governance and the work of the organization. Board members may be involved in some of the work, either in management or direct service functions. Staff and clients may have representation on the board. The organization may be described as being primarily staff-owned since members of the founding group often become the first staff and develop a culture of collective values in which staff exerts strong influence and even control.

B.   SELF-REGENERATING

The ownership structure of these organizations is simple: board members own the organization, are accountable primarily to themselves, and are responsible for ensuring that the board perpetuates itself. Self-regeneration may also typify some boards that present a slate of candidates to a membership, which then rubber-stamps the nominating slate in what might be considered a 'nominal' election.

C.   FUNDER APPOINTED

These are organizations (agencies) established to deliver a particular service or exercise a particular mandate on behalf of the funding agency, which is usually a federal, provincial or municipal government. The organizational form and purpose is determined by the legislation under which they are incorporated. Typical examples include crown agencies, health or social service authorities (e.g., the National Arts Centre, Ontario Community Care Access Centers, Alberta and B.C. Health Regions, the Alberta Mental Health Advisory Board, etc), libraries and museums. The funding authority holds the organization accountable for the delivery of a public benefit but is usually cautious in the exercise of its ultimate rights of 'ownership' except in the face of intense public controversy or serious deviation from the policy objectives of the funder.

D.   CHARTERED (AFFILIATE)

This organizational form is comprised of a provincial, national or international organization that establishes or creates local affiliates – chapters or branches – under the umbrella of the letters patent and bylaws of the provincial, national or international organization.

Examples include the Osteoporosis Society of Canada, service clubs and some churches. The central organization may operate with a self-regenerating board, with election of board members from individual members of the organization or elections based on some form of representation from the local chapters or entities.

Such organizations may also be incorporated under nonprofit corporations legislation and registered as charities. Lines of accountability can be quite diffuse.

E.   MEMBERSHIP ELECTED

i.   *Social/health co-operative*

This organizational form is primarily consumer-owned (unlike the collective which is primarily staff-owned). However, decision-making processes in smaller co-operatives may be much like those of collectives and, like collectives, are subject to some of the same vulnerabilities of growth and the need for increasing formalization. Boards that are elected by, and that represent the interests of, consumer members typically govern consumer cooperatives with larger memberships. Board structure and decision-making processes become more formal as the organization grows. Typical examples are housing, health and day care co-ops and support groups for parents with developmentally disabled children. Individual local incorporated or chartered religious groups also bear many of the characteristics of this model.

Co-operatives are defined as "autonomous associations of persons united voluntarily to meet their common economic, social and cultural needs and aspirations through a jointly-owned and democratically-controlled enterprise. Co-operatives are based on the values of self-help, self-responsibility, democracy, equality, equity and solidarity. They believe in the ethical values of honesty, openness, social responsibility and caring for others."[92] These values are incorporated in their code of ethics, which also values justice, diversity and professional service.

Co-operatives operate on seven principles or guidelines through which they put their values into practice:

1. voluntary and open membership;
2. democratic member control;
3. member economic participation;
4. autonomy and independence;
5. education, training and information;
6. co-operation among co-operatives; and
7. concern for community.

ii. Federated

This organizational form is an association of independent organizations that share a common mandate or common interests. 'Ownership' is vested in the member organizations and is exercised through a board of directors that is elected or appointed by that membership.

Members may be autonomous provincial/state or local branches/chapters of a provincial or national organization or organizations/associations with a common mandate or interest. The members elect or nominate representatives to the board. Typical examples include the Canadian AIDS Society, the Ontario Association of Children's Aid Societies and the Canadian Mental Health Association.

Federations may also be *Networks* or associations of other multi-member associations that formally constitute as a nonprofit network of organizations with a common interest. Their members may be some combination of associations and independent organizations.

F. CONSTITUENCY ELECTED

This may be either or both an organizational form and/or a board type (See Appendix A: Board types). Some organizations have a membership of individuals (or constituent groups) who have multiple, and potentially conflicting, stakeholder interests. This is similar to our form of parliamentary democracy. Membership is nominally open to anyone. The membership core of local nonprofits using this model is often made up of staff, volunteers, consumers, related professionals and members of the general public with a particular interest in the organization's work. Ongoing governance responsibilities are vested in a board of directors elected by the members from within the membership ranks.

G. PUBLICLY ELECTED

The most common example of this organizational form in the broader nonprofit sector is school boards. Some jurisdictions have also been exploring this approach for health authorities. A notable example of these is the province of Saskatchewan, where health authorities include a mix of both appointed and elected board members. Publicly elected boards have a heavier demand for accountability from their electors and are typically much more involved in operational matters than are organizations with other ownership structures. Collectives and smaller cooperatives are an evident exception.

H. MIXED SELECTION PROCESS

There are numerous examples of organizations that select their board primarily through one of the selection processes described above but that also combine this with one or more other methods of bringing on new board members. For example, Saskatchewan Health Authorities have some members appointed by government and others elected by the public. Until recently, the boards of Children's Aid Societies in Ontario were made up primarily of directors who were elected by members of the organization but there was also a requirement for a minimum number of municipally elected councilors appointed by the municipal Council. The local foster parent organization in most instances also nominated a representative, with full voting status, to the board.

Many hospital boards have municipal appointees. Multiple stakeholders including members elected from the public-at-large, users' committees and staff, select Quebec Regional Health and Social Services Boards. In some instances the board, municipality or Ministry may also appoint members.

Many nonprofit organizations, regardless of how board members are normally selected, also have a provision that allows the incumbent board to fill vacancies that occur mid-term or to appoint members-at-large.

APPENDIX C – BOARD EFFECTIVENESS QUICK CHECK

INSTRUCTIONS

The Quick Check is intended to be completed by board members and the CEO. Please rate each statement according to your perception of how well your organization/board attends to each of these factors. Ratings are on a seven-point scale where 5 equals 'Agree Strongly', 0 equals "Disagree Strongly'and Don't Know equals minus one (-1). Please enter in the line to the right of each statement the numerical rating that most closely corresponds to your perception of how well your board attends to each of the items. We are seeking an 'off-the-top-of-your-head' or spontaneous response based on your immediate perceptions.

Note: The term CEO is used to refer to chief executive officer, executive director, senior manager, management team leader, staff coordinator and other similar designations.

Rating Scale: Agree Strongly (5); Agree (4); Agree Somewhat (3); Disagree Somewhat (2); Disagree (1); Disagree Strongly (0); Don't Know (-1)

1. **This organization's orientation for board members adequately prepares them to fulfill their governance responsibilities.** _____

2. **This board is actively involved in planning the direction and priorities of the organization.** _____

3. **The board does a good job of evaluating the performance of the CEO** (*measuring results against objectives*). _____

4. **This organization is financially sound** (*viable and stable*). _____

5. **Board members demonstrate clear understanding of the respective roles of the board and CEO.** _____

6. **The organization's resources are used efficiently** (*good value for money spent*). _____

7. **The board has high credibility with key stakeholders** (*e.g., funders, donors, consumers, collateral organizations or professionals, community, staff*). _____

8. **Board members demonstrate commitment to this organization's mission and values.** _____

9. **Board members comply with requirements outlined in key elements of the governance structure** (*bylaws, policies, code of conduct, conflict of interest, traditional/cultural norms, etc.*). _____

10. **The board's capacity to govern effectively is not impaired by conflicts between members.** _____

11. **There is a productive working relationship between the board and the CEO** (*characterized by good communication and mutual respect*). _____

12. **I am confident that this board would effectively manage any organizational crisis that could be reasonably anticipated.** _____

13. **Board meetings are well managed.** _____

14. **The board uses sound decision-making processes** (*focused on board responsibilities, factual information, efficient use of time, items not frequently revisited, effective implementation*). _____

15. **This organization has a good balance between organizational stability and innovation.** _____

Total of the 15 items _____

Overall Score (**Total divided by 15**) _____

Board Effectiveness Quick Check — Scoring

Calculate the Overall Average for each respondent by totaling the ratings on the fifteen items and dividing by fifteen. Calculate the average of responses from individual board members on each of the fifteen individual items and the Overall Average by totaling the ratings of all board members and dividing by the number of board members who completed the 'Quick Check'. Compare the board averages to the responses of the CEO.

Item	A	B	C	D	E	F	G	H	I	J	K	L	M	N	O	Total	Avg. *	CEO **
1																		
2																		
3																		
4																		
5																		
6																		
7																		
8																		
9																		
10																		
11																		
12																		
13																		
14																		
15																		
Total																		
Total 15																		

* Total divided by number of BOARD respondents for each item. This provides the overall board effectiveness rating.

** *Compare average of board responses to CEO responses for each item and the total.*

Note: If you wish to compare the results of your board's responses to the 'Quick Check' with the average of those in our database, please contact the author. There is a small fee to cover the costs of this service.

Board Effectiveness Quick Check — Interpretation of Values

Please note that the interpretation of these scores should not be provided to the respondents in advance.

The following 'Values' suggest that the board governs:

5 – Very, Very Well. Can you believe it? The perfect nonprofit board!

4 – 5. A highly competent board. Congratulations!

4 – Very Well. A pretty competent board. Attention to a few key items should be rewarded with congratulations.

3 – 4. Conscientiously. A struggling board that's done some things well or very well but has some areas that need improvement. Fix what's broken before it gets worse. It's a slippery slope or a rocky climb. Are you on your way up or on your way down? Get outside help if the areas that need attention are board culture or board processes!

3 – Inconsistently. A board on the edge. Substantial improvements are needed now. Develop an action plan! This score is typical of boards that have paid some attention to structure and less to processes and organizational culture or vice versa, of boards in a critical transitional phase and of boards that are working to improve their governance effectiveness.

2 – 3. A board in need of a life raft. Values between 2 and 3 suggest either a uniformly poor pattern or a board that is doing some things moderately well and others very poorly. Outside assistance is needed to avoid a crisis, if it's not too late.

2 – Very Inconsistently. A board overboard. Time for a major overhaul. The board needs a complete external review of its governance functions, practices, information systems and membership.

1 – 2. A drowning board. An average value below 2 represents many items scored as 'Don't Know' or 'Disagree'. It indicates lack of attention to critical governance functions and serious default in due diligence and fiduciary responsibilities. The board should be seriously concerned about potential personal liability.

1 – Not at all. What has the board been doing? A board in need of a new captain and crew. Time to replace the board and CEO! Board and other key stakeholders should be alarmed. Funders should have intervened some time ago.

Please note that the items contained in this checklist are derived from research that suggests a correlation between good governance practices and organizational effectiveness.[91] The interpretations drawn here are based on a limited application of the 'Quick Check' to date and our best estimates of the significance of the values. If they do not concur with your own best judgment of the effectiveness of your board or organization, it should be considered a matter for further exploration with the author, rather than an occasion for despair or rejoicing.

Note: The Quick Check is also contained on the CD ROM available with volume purchases of this book.

CD ROM

Governing for Results: A Director's Guide to Good Governance

This CD ROM provides sample bylaws, governance policies, and committee terms of reference that may be readily adapted to your particular organization. It also contains copies of the self-assessment tools presented in this book.

Ordering Instructions

The CD ROM is available from the author, at a cost of $10.00 dollars for shipping and handling, upon confirmation of purchase of ten or more copies of this handbook The CD ROM may also be purchased directly from the author for $29.95 plus $10.00 shipping and handling. Please contact the author at mel.gill@synergyassociates.ca for payment and ordering instructions.

REFERENCES

Allison, Michael (2002) "Into the Fire: Boards and Executive Transitions" *Nonprofit Management and Leadership* 12 (4) 341-351

Auditor General of British Columbia (1999/2000) "A Review of the Fast Ferry Project: Governance and Risk Management." Report 5, cited in Gill 2001.

Auditor General of Canada www.oag-bvg.gc.ca, Canada site, provinces & territories

Asian Development Bank (1998) Annual Report www.adb.org.

Block, Stephen R., Perfect Nonprofit Boards: Myths, Paradoxes, and Paradigms, Needham Heights, Simon & Schuster, Massachusetts, 1998 (138 pages)

Bradshaw, P., Murray, V., & Wolpin, J. (1992). "Do nonprofit boards make a difference? An exploration of the relationships among board structure, process and effectiveness." *Nonprofit and Voluntary Sector Quarterly* 21(13) 227-249.

Broadbent, Hon. Edward, Chair, Panel on Accountability and Governance in the Voluntary Sector. "Building on Strength: Improving Governance and Accountability in Canada's Voluntary Sector" (Broadbent Report) Ottawa, 1999. (121 pages)

Broder, Peter, Coordinating Editor. (2002) Primer For Directors Of Not-For-Profit Corporations: Rights, Duties and Practices. Industry Canada. (99 pages)

Brown, D., Brown, D., & Birkbeck, K. (1998). "Canadian directorship practices 1997: A quantum leap in governance". Ottawa: Conference Board of Canada.

Brudney, J. L., and Murray, V. (1998) "Do Intentional Efforts to Improve Boards Really Work? The Views of Nonprofit CEOs". *Nonprofit Management and Leadership, 8(4) Summer 1998, 333—348*

Buchanan, Phil (2004) "Foundation Governance: The CEO Viewpoint" The Center for Effective Philanthropy. http://www.effectivephilanthropy.com/images/pdfs/governanceceoview.pdf

Buckingham, Marcus & Coffman, Curt (1999). First, Break all the Rules: What the world's greatest managers do differently. New York: Simon & Schuster. (269 pages)

Cadbury, Sir A. (1992). "Report of the Committee on Financial Aspects of Corporate Governance", London Stock Exchange, HMSO.

California's School to Work Interagency Transition Partnership (1999) "Using consensus for decision making" http://www.sna.com'switp/onsen.html,13/10/99

Canada Corporations Act, R.S.C. 1970, c. C-32 (See also Canada Not-for-Profit Corporations Act, C-21 tabled for parliamentary review, First Reading, Nov. 15, 2004. http://www.parl.gc.ca/38/1/parlbus/chambus/house/bills/government/C-21/C-21_1/C-21_cover-E.html)

Carver, John (1990) Boards That Make a Difference Jossey-Bass, San Francisco. (272 pages)

CICA (2000) "Guidance for Directors: Dealing with Risk in the Boardroom" Control, Risk and Governance – Vol. 4, April 2000, Canadian Institute of Chartered Accountants, Toronto

Collins, James C. and Porras, Jerry I. (1994). Built to Last. Harper Collins, New York. (320 pages)

Cornerstones of Community: Highlights of the National Survey of Nonprofit and Voluntary Organizations. Statistics Canada (2004) Minister of Industry, Ottawa, Catalogue no. 61-533-XPE

CRA (Canada Revenue Agency) (2003) Policy Statement, Political Activities. http://www.cra-arc.gc.ca/tax/charities/policy/cps/cps-022-e.html#P147_14872

Cutt, James and Murray, Vic (2000) Accountability and Effectiveness Evaluation in Nonprofit Organizations, Routledge, New York. (294 pages)

Demb, A. and Nuebauer, F.F. (1992) The Corporate Board: Confronting the Paradoxes. Oxford University Press, New York. (232 pages)

"Designing and Facilitating Groups in Conflict" Canadian Institute for Conflict Resolution (CICR). Ottawa, www.cicr-icrc.ca/main_e.html

Dey, Peter, (1994) Chair, Toronto Stock Exchange Committee on Corporate Governance in Canada. "Where Were the Directors? Guidelines for Improved Corporate Governance in Canada" (Dey Report) Toronto.

Drucker, Peter, "Lessons for Successful Nonprofit Governance", *Nonprofit Management and Leadership"*, 1990 1 (1), 7-14.

Duca, Diane J., Nonprofit Boards: Roles, Responsibilities, and Performance, John Wiley, New York, 1996 (179 pages)

Fletcher, Kathleen (2002) "Themes Across Cases of Non-Conventional Governance: A Preliminary Report from the Discovery Phase of the Governance Futures Project" Paper presented at ARNOVA conference, Montreal 2002.

Francis, Fred and Francis, Peg (2003) Democratic Rules of Order Seventh Edition, Francis, Victoria, B. C. (72 pages)

Gibelman, Margaret, Gelman, Sheldon R. and Pollack, Daniel (1997) "The Credibility of Nonprofit Boards: A View from the 1990s and Beyond" *Administration in Social Work, 21(2),* Hawthorne Press Inc.

Gill, Mel. (2001) "Governance Do's and Don'ts: Practical Lessons from Case Studies on Twenty Canadian Nonprofits" Institute On Governance, Ottawa, Canada, www.synergyassociates.ca, Publications.

Gill, Mel (2002). "Building effective approaches to governance". *The Nonprofit Quarterly, 9:* 46-49.

Gill, Mel, Flynn, Robert and Reissing, Elke. (2005) "The Governance Self-Assessment Checklist" *Nonprofit Management and Leadership* Vol. 15:3

Golensky, Martha (2000) "Does Motivation Matter? An Exploratory Study of the Relationship Between Incentives for Board Participation and Board Performance" Paper presented at the 'Innovation, Change and Continuity in Nonprofit Organization Governance' conference, April 6-7, Kansas City Missouri. http://www.nonprofitbasics.org/PDF/Article6.PDF

Gray, J. (2002). "The best and worst boards in Canada". *Canadian Business,* August 19, 29–35.

Green, J.C., & Griesinger, D.W. (1996). "Board performance and organizational effectiveness in nonprofit social service organizations". *Nonprofit Management and Leadership, 6,* 381-402.

Hamilton, John P. (2001) "Liability of Directors". Volunteer Lawyers Service www.volunteerlawyers.org.

Herman, R. D., & Renz, D. O. (1997). "Multiple constituencies and the social construction of nonprofit organization effectiveness." *Nonprofit and Voluntary Sector Quarterly* 26(2) 185-206

Herman, R. D., & Renz, D. O. (1998). "Nonprofit organizational effectiveness: Contrasts between especially effective and less effective organizations". *Nonprofit Management and Leadership, 9(1),* 23-38.

Herman, R. D., & Renz, D. O. (2000). "Board practices of especially effective and less effective local nonprofit organizations". *American Review of Public Administration, 30(2),* 142-160.

Herman, R. D., & Renz, D. O. (2002). "Nonprofit organizational effectiveness: practical implications of research on an elusive concept." Occasional Paper (1-16) www.bloch.umkc.edu/ cookingham. Forthcoming, *Public Administration Review* "Doing Things Right and Effectiveness in Local Nonprofit Organizations: A Panel Study".

Holland, Thomas P. (2002) "Board Accountability: Lessons from the Field" *Nonprofit Management and Leadership*, 12(4) 409-428.

Holland, Thomas P. and Jackson, Douglas K. (1998) "Strengthening board performance: findings and lessons from demonstration projects". *Nonprofit Management and Leadership*, 9(2) 121-134

Hospital Reports, Ontario Hospital Association. Hospital Report 2003 Series (January 2004) http://www.oha.com/oha/reprt5.nsf

Houle, Cyril O., <u>Governing Boards: Their Nature and Nurture</u>, Jossey-Bass Publishers, San Francisco, 1989 (184 pages)

Howe, Fisher. <u>Welcome to the Board: Your Guide to Effective Participation</u>. Jossey-Bass, San Francisco, 1995 (110 pages)

Jackson, D. K., & Holland, T. P. (1998). "Measuring the effectiveness of nonprofit boards". *Nonprofit and Voluntary Sector Quarterly, 27(2)*, 159-182.

Kaplan, Robert S. and Norton, David P. (1996). <u>The Balance Scorecard – Translating Strategy into Action</u>. Harvard Business Press. (323 pages)

Kids First: Preserving Families for Children. Corporate Plan, Children's Aid Society of Ottawa-Carleton, 1993

King, Norman, Lan, George, McMahon, Sharon & Singh, Jang, University of Windsor, in Gill, Mel. (2001) "Governance Do's and Don'ts: Practical Lessons from Case Studies on Twenty Canadian Nonprofits" Institute On Governance, Ottawa, Canada, www.synergyassociates.ca, Publications.

Kramer, R. M. (1985) "Toward a contingency model of board-executive relations." *Administration in Social Work, 9(3:15-33),* Hawthorne Press Inc.

Leighton, David S. R. and Thain, Donald H. (1997) <u>Making Boards Work: What Directors Must Do To Make Canadian Boards Effective</u>. McGraw-Hill Ryerson Ltd., Whitby. (296 pages)

Letts, Christine W., Ryan, William P. and Grossman, Allen (1999) <u>High Performance Nonprofit Organizations: Managing Upstream for Greater Impact</u>. John Wiley & Sons Inc. New York. (207 pages)

Light, Mark. <u>The Strategic Board: The Step-by-Step Guide to High Impact Governance</u>. John Wiley & Sons, New York, 2001. (232 pages)

Mintzberg, Henry (1994) "The Rise and Fall of Strategic Planning" *Harvard Business Review* 72(1) 107-114

Nobbie, Patricia Dautel & Brudney, Jeffrey L. "Testing the Implementation, Board Performance and Organizational Effectiveness of the Policy Governance Model in Nonprofit Boards of Directors." *Nonprofit and Voluntary Sector Quarterly*, December 2003, 32:4. 571-595

Online Business Women's Center." http://www.onlinewbc.gov/docs/finance/fs

Plantz, Margaret C., Greenway, Martha T. and Hendreicks, Michael (1997) "Outcome Measurement: Showing Results in the Nonprofit Sector" United Way of America, www.unitedway.org/outcomes/library/prmomres.cfm.

"Privacy Policy". Canadian Centre for Philanthropy, www.ccp.ca.

Renz, David O. (2004) "An Overview of Nonprofit Governance" adapted from a chapter prepared for <u>Philanthropy in America: A Comprehensive Historical Encyclopedia</u> (2004) Dwight Burlingame, ed. ABC-CLIO http://bsbpa.umkc.edu/mwcnl//board%20resources/intro.htm

Renz, David O. "Consent Agenda". A Board Resource Tool from the Midwest Center for Nonprofit Leadership. www.bloch.umkc.edu/cookingham.

"Resources For Accountability and Financial Management in the Voluntary Sector" (2003) VSI (Voluntary Sector Initiative) http://www.vsi-isbc.ca/eng/funding/financial_guide/index.cfm.

Robert, Henry Martyn (2000) <u>Robert's Rules of Order Newly Revised</u>, 10th Edition, Perseus Publishers. www.robertsrules.com.

Robinson, Maureen K., <u>Nonprofit Boards That Work: The End of One-Size-Fits-All Governance</u>, John Wiley & Sons, 2001 (154 pages)

Sarbancs-Oxley Act of 2002: Public Company Accounting and Investor Protection Act. 107th Congress of the United States of America.

Schacter, Mark (2002) "Not a Tool Kit: Practitioner's Guide to Measuring the Performance of Public Programs" Institute On Governance, Ottawa

Senge, Peter M. (1990) <u>The Fifth Discipline: The Art and Practice of the Learning Organization</u>. Doubleday, New York. (423 pages)

Tam, Pauline "Less tolerant, more wary of door-to-door solicitors." The Ottawa Citizen, March 04, 2004

Taylor, Barbara E., Chait, Richard P. and Holland, Thomas P. (1996) "The New Work of the Nonprofit Board." *Harvard Business Review*. 74:36-47.

"The New Nonprofit Almanac: In Brief: Facts and Figures on the Independent Sector" (2001) Independent Sector.

Trout, Stran L., PRP. http://www.newkent.net/rules.html.

Tsui, Anne S (1984). "A Role Set of Analysis of Managerial Reputation" *Organizational Behavior and Human Performance* 34(1) 64-96.

Tweeten, Byron L. (2002) <u>Transformational Boards: A Practical Guide to Engaging Your Board and Embracing Change</u>. Jossey-Bass, San Francisco. (191 pages)

United Way of America (1996) "Measuring Program Outcomes: A Practical Approach" United Way of America, Alexandria, VA. www.unitedway.org/outcomes/library/pgmomres.cfm.

Widmer, Candace and Houchin, Susan (2001) <u>The Art of Trusteeship: The Nonprofit Board Member's Guide to Effective Governance</u>, Jossey-Bass, San Francisco. (208 pages)

Wolfensberger, Wolf. (1984) "Voluntary Associations on Behalf of Societally Devalued and/or

Handicapped People" National Institute on Mental Retardation, York University, Toronto.

Wood, Miriam M.. (1992) "Is Governing Board Behavior Cyclical?" *Nonprofit Management and Leadership,* Winter 1992:3(2) 139-161.

Wood, Miriam M., Editor (1996) Nonprofit Boards and Leadership: Cases on Governance, Change and Board-Staff Dynamics. Jossey-Bass Inc. San Francisco. (239 pages)

Zimmerman, Brenda, Lindberg, Curt and Plsek, Paul. Edgeware: insights from complexity science for health care leaders. VHA Inc. Irving Texas, 1998. (226 pages)

ENDNOTES

1 Gill, Governance Do's and Don'ts: Practical Lessons from Case Studies on Twenty Canadian Nonprofits, Institute On Governance 2001

2 Ibid.

3 Case Illustrations are drawn from case summaries reported in Gill, op.cit. 2001 unless otherwise noted.

4 Renz, An Overview of Nonprofit Governance. 2004:1

5 Adapted from Asian Development Bank. 1998

6 Cornerstones of Community: Highlights of the National Survey of Nonprofit and Voluntary Organizations. Statistics Canada, Minister of Industry 2004:9-21

7 Broadbent, Panel on Accountability. 1999:13

8 The New Nonprofit Almanac 2001:3-9

9 Auditor General of Canada, www.oag-bvg.gc.ca, Canada Report

10 Bradshaw, Murray & Wolpin (1992); Green & Greisinger (1996); Herman & Renz (1998, 2000, 2002); Jackson & Holland (1998); Holland, et. al. (1998); Letts, et. al. (1999); Gill, et. al. 2005

11 Brown, et. al. Canadian directorship practices. Conference Board of Canada 1997:3-4

12 Gray, The best and worst boards in Canada. Canadian Business 2002:29–35

13 Houle, Governing Boards: Their Nature and Nurture. Jossey-Bass 1989:5

14 Ibid. p.86

15 Gill, Building effective approaches to governance. The Nonprofit Quarterly 2002:47

16 Bradshaw, et. al., Do nonprofit boards make a difference? Nonprofit and Voluntary Sector Quarterly 1992:243-44

17 Golensky, Does Motivation Matter? Occasional paper 2000:18

18 Collins and Porras, Built to Last. Harper Collins 1994:8

19 Broadbent, op. cit. 1999:119

20 Adapted from Broder, Primer For Directors Of Not-For-Profit Corporations. Industry Canada 2002:15-28; See also Hamilton, 2001 Liability of Directors. Volunteer Lawyers Service, www.volunteerlawyers.org

21 Ibid. pp.31-45

22 Carver, Boards That Make a Difference. Jossey-Bass 1990

23 Gill, op.cit. 2001

24 Gill, et.al. "The Governance Self-Assessment Checklist" *Nonprofit Management and Leadership 2005*

25 Wood, Is Governing Board Behavior Cyclical? Nonprofit Management and Leadership 1992:139-161; and Nonprofit Boards and Leadership, Jossey-Bass 1996

26 Gill, et. al., op.cit. 2005

27 Nobbie and Brudney, Testing the Implementation, Board Performance and Organizational Effectiveness of the Policy Governance Model in Nonprofit Boards of Directors. Nonprofit and Voluntary Sector Quarterly 2003

28 Gill, op.cit. 2002:49

29 Gill, op.cit. 2001

30 Carver, op.cit. 1990

31 Broder, op.cit. 2002:64

32 Demb and Neubauer, The Corporate Board: Confronting the Paradoxes. Oxford University Press 1992:5-7

33 Gill, op.cit. 2001; Taylor, et. al. The New Work of the Nonprofit Board. Harvard Business Review. 1996:74:36-47

34 Gill, et. al., op.cit. 2005

35 Gill, op.cit. 2001

36 Carver, op.cit. 1990:35

37 Bradshaw, et. al., Do nonprofit boards make a difference? Nonprofit and Voluntary Sector Quarterly 1992

38 Collins and Poras, op.cit. 1994:9

39 Zimmerman, et. al., Edgeware. VHA Inc. 1998:26-27

40 Mintzberg, The Rise and Fall of Strategic Planning. Harvard Business Review 1994:110

41 Collins and Porras, op.cit. 1994:73

42 Ibid. 1994:73

43 Kids First: Preserving Families for Children. Corporate Plan, Children's Aid Society of Ottawa-Carleton, 1993

44 Ibid. 1994:75

45 See Widmer and Houchin, The Art of Trusteeship. Jossey-Bass 2001:69-82 'Developing Funds' for a more thorough discussion on this subject.

46 Gibelman, et. al. The Credibility of Nonprofit Boards. Administration in Social Work, Hawthorne Press 1997:25

47 Buckingham and Coffman, First, Break all the Rules. Simon & Schuster 1999

48 Ibid.

49 Allison, Into the Fire: Boards and Executive Transitions. Nonprofit Management and Leadership 2002:12(4)341-351

50 Taylor, et. al. The New Work of the Nonprofit Board. Harvard Business Review 1996:74:37

51 CRA, 2003 Policy Statement, Political Activities

52 Tam, Less tolerant, more wary of door-to-door solicitors. The Ottawa Citizen, March 04, 2004

53 CICA, Guidance for Directors: Dealing with Risk in the Boardroom. Canadian Institute of Chartered Accountants 2000:2

54 Broder, op. cit. 2002:4

55 Sarbanes-Oxley Act of 2002 and Dey Report, TSE Guidelines for Corporate Governance

56 Kramer, 1985 in Gibelman, et. al. The Credibility of Nonprofit Boards. Administration in Social Work 1997:21(2)24

57 Taylor, et. al., op. cit. 1996:36

58 Drucker, Lessons for Successful Nonprofit Governance. Nonprofit Management and Leadership, 1990:1(1)8

59 Gill, et. al., op. cit. 2005

60 Zimmerman et. al., op. cit. 1998:136-140. The 'Stacey Agreement and Certainty Matrix'

61 CICA, op. cit. 2000:2

62 California's School to Work Interagency Transition Partnership, 1999

63 Senge, <u>The Fifth Discipline</u>. Doubleday 1990

64 Fletcher, Themes Across Cases of Non-Conventional Governance: A Preliminary Report from the Discovery Phase of the Governance Futures Project. Occasional paper, ARNOVA 2002

65 Buckingham and Coffman, op. cit. 1999:28

66 Gill, et. al., op. cit. 2005

67 Holland, Board Accountability. Nonprofit Management and Leadership 2002:12(4) 409-428

68 Taylor, et. al., op. cit. 1996:36

69 Gill, op. cit. 2001

70 See Renz, Consent Agenda. Midwest Center for Nonprofit Leadership for more detailed guidance on this.

71 Robert, <u>Robert's Rules of Order Newly Revised</u>, 10th Edition, Perseus Publishers 2002

72 Francis, <u>Democratic Rules of Order</u> Seventh Edition 2003

73 Trout, PRP http://www.newkent.net/rules.html

74 Kids First, op. cit.1993

75 Herman & Renz, Multiple Constituencies. Nonprofit and Voluntary Sector Quarterly 1997 and 'Board Practices' American Review of Public Administration 2002

76 Herman & Renz, Nonprofit organizational effectiveness: practical implications of research on an elusive concept. 2002:13

77 Carver, op. cit. 1990:35

78 Plantz, et. al. Outcome Measurement: Showing Results in the Nonprofit Sector. United Way of America 1997

79 Cutt and Murray, <u>Accountability and Effectiveness Evaluation in Nonprofit Organizations</u>. Routledge 2000

80 Schacter, Not a Tool Kit. Institute On Governance 2002

81 Measuring Program Outcomes. United Way of America 1996

82 Plantz, et. al., op. cit.

83 Schacter, op. cit. 2002:10

84 Ibid.

85 Ibid.

86 Schacter, op. cit. 2002:25

87 Kaplan and Norton, <u>The Balanced Scorecard</u>. Harvard Business Press 1996

88 Hospital Reports, 2003 Series. Ontario Hospital Association 2004

89 Carver, op. cit. 1990:28

90 Carver, op. cit. 1990:193

91 Gill, et. al. op. cit.

92 Canadian Cooperative Association, http://www.coopscanada.coop/aboutcoop/

ABOUT THE AUTHOR

Mel Gill, is President of Synergy Associates, Consultants in Governance and Organizational Development, Ottawa, Canada. He has a B.A. in political science, psychology and economics from the University of Saskatchewan and an M.S.W. from Dalhousie University in Halifax.

Mel spent 17 years in the Saskatchewan public service in a variety of front-line, policy and senior management positions. His responsibilities included development and management of standards and funding criteria for community service and employment grants to voluntary sector organizations and private sector employers, as well as implementation of Program-Based Management Information Systems in several government departments, as a Senior Analyst with the Treasury Board.

Mel served for 12 years as executive director of one of the largest nonprofit social service organizations in Canada. He has also served as a member of a score of local, national and provincial voluntary sector boards. Since 1999 he has been conducting research, writing and consulting in the voluntary and broader public sectors. He is also the author of several journal articles.

Contact Information:

Phone: (613) 837-8757

Fax: (613) 837-1431

E-mail: mel.gill@synergyassociates.ca

www.governance.synergyassociates.ca

ISBN 1-41204938-5